In memory of my mother
who gave up cigarettes for me
with love

ACKNOWLEDGEMENTS

I would like to thank the following people for their invaluable help: Gloria Ferris, my agent, for her constant support; Kyle Cathie, my publisher, who shares my enthusiasm for the book; Annie Jackson, my editor, who did such a marvellous job with wisdom and always good humour; Geoff Hayes, for his super cover design; my dear father who loves everything I write unreservedly; and my sister, Wendy, my most ardent supporter and friend, for her love and encouragement.

CONTENTS

INTRODUCTION

Quiz No. 1

If you answer 'yes' to three or more of the following questions you need this book:

1. Do you ever say 'I'd give up but I don't want to put on weight'?

2. Have you ever lost weight and put it all back on again?

3. Do you regularly make New Year resolutions to:
   i) give up smoking?
      and/or
   ii) lose weight once and for all?

4. Have you tried to diet or give up smoking and failed?

5. Do you see yourself as weak-willed?

6. Do you procrastinate?

7. Have you ever tried to lose weight for a special occasion?

8. Has anyone ever said your hair or breath smelt of cigarettes?

9. Do you really want to give up smoking successfully?

Don't despair – help is at hand. The aim of my book is to show how you **need** not put on weight whilst giving up smoking and how you will become healthy and fit as well. I hope it will help anyone who wants to **improve the quality of their life**, get the best out of every day and prevent themselves and their family falling ill. It should be read by anyone who **genuinely wants to give up smoking** ... **and not become fat when they do**.

I decided, when I gave up smoking my 40–50 cigarettes a day, that not only was I not going to get fat but I was not going to become neurotic about my eating habits either. I made up my mind that I wanted to eat well, enjoy my food, take up some exercise which I enjoyed and generally lead a well-balanced life.

All I can tell you is – it worked ...

The most difficult part was giving up cigarettes. I had to break the addiction of habit and replace it with new healthy habits. I'm not pretending it was a bowl of cherries, but bit by bit it got easier, and day by day I began to feel there was an end in sight. The not-putting-on-too-much-weight part was so much easier than the giving-up-smoking part. After all, when you give up cigarettes there's no either/or about it. When you want to lose or maintain your weight you do always have a choice. You don't have to eat cream cakes, you can choose a delicious piece of fruit instead – the choice is yours. The feeling you get after you've made the right choice is even better still – when you realize you haven't blown it!

My healthy eating and exercise plan is going to fit in with you and not the other way round. It's not some formula of wonder-drinks or magic potions which would disrupt your way of life. The changes you need to make to have a healthy, balanced lifestyle are very minor.

You'll be choosing slow-release foods, which are those high in fibre, and which keep energy levels high for longest but which also give you variety and taste. You'll be choosing your foods from wholemeal and wholegrain cereals, bread, pasta, rice, dried peas and beans, pulses, nuts and breakfast cereals. You'll be eating oily fish at least three times a week – more if you like it and chicken (without the skin), but no red meat. You'll be eating five or six portions of fruit and vegetables daily – as much of it as you can raw. You'll be eating complex carbohydrates at every meal, i.e. bread, potatoes, rice, pasta or cereals – wholegrain or wholemeal. You'll be eating low-fat dairy produce and only polyunsaturated oils and spreads, best of which are ones containing olive oil which can also be used for cooking.

In addition, you'll be increasing the amount of exercise you take – anything from a brisk walk, swimming, or cycling to something more strenuous like tennis or squash. Hopefully this will become a way of life, but you *must* choose a sport that you enjoy.

So make up your mind to change and **do it now**. I'm glad I did.

Chapter 1

KICKING THE HABIT

You probably would not have picked up this book if you didn't, in your heart of hearts, feel you *should* stop smoking.

So just to reinforce that, let's remind ourselves of some of the facts and figures.

A report published in May 1992 states that by 1995 smoking will kill one person in five. UK government figures show that there are still 13 million smokers in Great Britain, 31% of men to 29% of women, and in 1990 men consumed 118 cigarettes weekly compared to women's 97. A frightening statistic is that 25% of 15-year-olds smoke, and many of them smoke 10 cigarettes a day. There are 10 million ex-smokers, and there is a definite trend towards people wanting to give up.

You would think that the alarming statistics below would be enough to kick-start smokers into giving up.

The fact that:

- one in eight smokers dies from heart disease

- one in three of all cancer deaths is smoking-related

- one in ten smokers develops lung cancer

- one in five smokers suffers from bronchitis

- smokers run an increased risk of stomach ulcers

- pregnant women who smoke are more likely to have underweight babies and premature births

- children are more vulnerable to chest infections, coughs and colds if they live with smokers
- women who smoke are twice as likely to develop cervical cancer as smoking seems to reduce the efficiency of the immune system in the cervix
- tobacco is responsible for around 30% of all deaths caused by cancer
- tobacco is one of the major causes of coronary heart disease; your poor heart has to work much harder as carbon monoxide (a poisonous gas) is released each time you smoke. This gas drastically curtails the oxygen level needed to carry the blood round the body to your heart
- passive smoking (breathing in other people's smoke) increases the risk of getting lung cancer, even in people who do not smoke themselves
- smokers risk suffering from blood clots caused by inhaling the poisonous nicotine, which also sends your blood pressure soaring and makes your heart beat faster each time you light up

For dog lovers

Here's a sobering fact for all dog-lovers, too: it has been proved (in research at Colorado State University, USA) that short- or medium-length nosed dogs are twice as likely to die from cancer if their owners are smokers.

In addition to these grim statistics, smoking:

- makes your hair reek
- gives you smelly breath
- irritates your eyes, making them water; makes wearing contact lenses difficult
- gives you a bad throat and makes you cough

- makes your voice hoarse
- makes your home reek of stale smoke
- makes your office stink
- ruins your meal in restaurants (and those of people at neighbouring tables)
- mars your enjoyment in the cinema
- causes headaches
- causes bronchitis and emphysema
- blocks nasal passages
- spoils your outings with friends who smoke
- spoils your day at the beach
- causes many an argument and creates bad feelings, second only to opposing views on politics and/or religion!
- makes your car unpleasant to travel in, even with all the windows open

Faced with all that evidence, *why* do we put off giving it up? There are several reasons:

1. Nicotine is an addictive drug.

2. Habit is an addictive drug.

3. The ritual that goes with smoking is comforting.

4. The thought of having nothing to do with your hands if you give up is unbearable.

5. The being 'one of the crowd' is important.

   But by far the most over-riding reason is:

6. Our fear of putting on weight.

The reason that people often put on weight when they stop smoking is that nicotine stimulates the production of a chemical called serotonin in your body, which creates feelings of calm and happiness. When you stop smoking your serotonin levels can be kept high by increasing the amount of carbohydrates you eat. Most people giving up cigarettes consume about 300 extra calories a day for at least four weeks.

And what is four weeks? Surely less time than you invested in your last wonder diet . . . ? In Chapter 7 I've given you sample menus for those difficult first four weeks, showing wholesome and delicious ways of consuming the extra 300 calories, without resorting to the biscuits or bar of chocolate when the craving takes you.

If you can't bear the thought of even *maybe* consuming 300 extra calories a day (and there's certainly no need to do so) why not increase your exercise level during this time? (For more about exercise – see Chapter 4.)

So, don't worry, it is normal to eat more than usual when you first stop smoking, but it will only be temporary. It may be that you are feeling really hungry for the first time in a long while as you begin to taste and smell food properly!

So now that we've established that it really is OK to put on a *few* pounds when you stop smoking, why not quit today?

My five golden rules

To make life easier, I have five golden rules which I refer to throughout this book. Here they are:

- **Do it now**
- **Be prepared**
- **Work at your own pace**
- **Don't aim for perfection**
- **Sort out your priorities**

***

DO IT NOW

Don't despair, don't procrastinate. Remember: when you give up cigarettes, you don't smoke. It's that simple.

Not so with eating. You don't have to go without. Quite the opposite, in fact. You just have to make decisions about which foods to eat. I'll show you how in Chapter 6. The secret lies in **being prepared**.

BE PREPARED

This is the key to the whole enchilada – if you're not prepared, you will never succeed. It is vital that, when faced with temptation, the solution is there at your fingertips.

WORK AT YOUR OWN PACE

If the thought of reading this book puts you off from even trying, why not dip into one or two chapters? But don't procrastinate . . . **do it now**!

DON'T AIM FOR PERFECTION

You are not in a competition with anybody else. Don't be too hard on yourself. There are lots of bonuses in changing your way of life. Why not dip into the chapter called 'Be Your Own Psychiatrist', page 60?

SORT OUT YOUR PRIORITIES

Most people's priorities, if they think seriously about it, are:

- to stay healthy

   and

- to be happy

and giving up smoking and eating well must surely be one of the best ways of contributing to both these priorities.

Keep telling yourself that, just as when you're poor you can't afford to replace old and broken possessions, so, if you're ill from smoking, you can't replace your health. Don't live to regret it.

Stopping smoking

1. Do it now.

2. Choose the day that you're going to stop smoking and tell just about every person you know – so that the incentive will be well and truly planted.

3. Give it up in one go rather than gradually, because otherwise, if you're at all like me, you'll tend to become too self-indulgent and keep giving yourself reasons why you should have 'just one more'!

4. **Throw away every single one of your remaining cigarettes** and that includes all the hidden ones you've stashed away!

5. Ask everyone not to sabotage your efforts.

6. Be strong. If someone offers you a cigarette, just say firmly, 'No, thanks, I don't smoke any more' or 'I've given them up.'

Congratulations, you're half-way there. Here are some hints to help start you off on the first day of your campaign to lead a better quality life:

• If another member of your family tries to give it up at the same time you'll have mutual support at all hours of the day or night, and you'll certainly understand each other's moods and irritability.

- It must also be said that it's easier if you live on your own because you won't be tempted by anyone else's smoke or, indeed, anyone trying to undermine your efforts. People often do if they're feeling guilty themselves.

So do try – it'll be worth it.

When you're feeling low

When you're feeling low and perhaps annoyed with your-self, it's good to remember that smoking has nothing to do with character – you are *not* weak but if you were unlucky enough to have taken up smoking, you've got a problem now, albeit a temporary one.

Here are a few bonuses to think about:

1. You're not endangering the lives of the rest of your family, your children and your pets.

2. You'll have greater immunity against coughs and colds.

3. You are not wasting money buying packs of cigarettes to induce illness.

4. You will have a nice-smelling home, workplace and car that other people will enjoy, too.

5. You won't suffer from smoker's bad breath and your hair and clothes will be smoke-free as well.

6. Your senses of taste and smell will be keener.

7. You'll have more energy.

8. You'll feel in control now that you're not going to be dependent on cigarettes.

9. You can sit where you choose in cinemas, restaurants and anywhere where smokers are segregated.

10. You don't have to rush out from a non-smoking meeting to take a few puffs in the corridor, the loo, or the street.

Remember: It's never too late to give up.

Let's be honest, there will be a few disadvantages to giving up but they will be *temporary* hurdles and soon you'll be up and running . . .

Withdrawal symptoms can manifest themselves in the following ways, but they may not, and they certainly won't last long:

1. Rowing and bickering with your nearest and dearest.

2. Being overly critical.

3. Causing unnecessary arguments with colleagues.

4. Finding it hard to concentrate.

5. Being irritable and restless.

Don't use these as reasons for not trying.

Your nearest and dearest will, no doubt, understand what you're going through, especially if they're joining you in the campaign. When you feel a row coming on, go for a walk – or excuse yourself in advance – you'll find people are only too willing to help at the thought of *not* having a smoker in their midst. Your concentration will return . . . especially if you feel you're going to be usurped at the office! If you are irritable and restless, you'll find plenty of ideas of what to do with yourself in the chapter on exercise, page 54.

Not everyone can manage to give up smoking by relying just on their own willpower. There are various ways you can get help. Nicotine chewing gum, acupuncture, hypnotism – whatever works for you is fine. But do it – NOW. Book a course, make that appointment, buy that first packet of gum – NOW.

Just a word about the different methods of alternative therapies you could try.

Acupuncture

Fine needles are inserted at strategic points on the body by the acupuncturist, to help patients regain optimum health and release blocked energy. The treatment includes helping withdrawal symptoms, anxiety and depression. The plus factor with acupuncture is that it releases endorphins – as does exercise, see page 54.

Hypnotherapy

A hypnotherapist will put you in a trance and then convince you that you have an aversion to cigarettes, or she or he may suggest a less radical step of giving up gradually. These two approaches might help some people kick the habit but I imagine that most successful are the people who already have the highest motivation to give up the habit permanently.

You could try your own 'aversion' therapy by buying only cigarettes which you dislike! You might get fed up with both the taste and the expense of this ruse.

Don't, however, be lulled into thinking that just because you want to be slim, fit and healthy, you can go to a hypnotherapist to work wonders. There are no short cuts and you will still have to eat healthily and take lots of exercise.

Shiatsu

This is similar to acupuncture in that finger pressure is applied to certain parts of the body to release energy. A useful side-effect to the treatment is the resultant feeling of calm, relaxation and tranquillity.

Aromatherapy

This massaging with essential oils is said to reduce stress and help relaxation, and is advocated for people who whilst suffering tension would benefit from human touch. Likewise herbalism – treatments made from plants – is beneficial to conditions caused by stress.

It is worth emphasising that if you are going to try one of these therapies, you must go to a fully trained and registered practitioner. I give below some useful bodies who will advise you:

Council for Complementary and Alternative Medicine, 19a Cavendish Square, London W1M 9AD. Tel: 071 409 1440

The Health Information Service. Tel: 0345 678 444

The Shiatsu Society, 14 Oakdene Road, Redhill, Surrey RH1 6BT. Tel: 0737 767896

The British Homeopathic Association, 27a Devonshire Street, London W1N 1RJ. Tel: 071 935 2163

Register of Qualified Aromatherapists. Tel: 071 263 2004

The Tisserand Association for Holistic Aromatherapists, 65 Church Road, Hove, East Sussex. Tel: 0273 206640

British Acupuncture Association, 34 Alderney Street, London SW1V 4EU. Tel: 071 834 1012

Council for Acupuncture, 179 Gloucester Place, London NW1 6DX. Tel: 071 724 5756

National Institute of Medical Herbalists, 9 Palace Gate, Exeter, Devon. Tel: 0392 426022

Women and smoking

It is far more difficult for women to give up smoking than men for the following reasons. Women are taught not to be aggressive and therefore often take out their feelings on themselves. Instead of shouting at someone they'll take the 'nice' way out and pop a cigarette in their mouths to calm their nerves. Women, particularly those at home and/or with small children, have to focus on the 'immediate' – in other words they have to cope with crying children, the house, waiting for the baby to wake up, waiting for their husbands to come home. They are always waiting for something to happen, as opposed to being able to make it happen, thus tremendous boredom and stress can surround them all day long and they smoke to alleviate both. If the house revolves around the mother/wife and everyone is dependent upon her and doesn't relish seeing her in a bad mood or unable to cope, they may say they would rather she smoked and kept her sanity – encouraging her not to give up smoking and become irritable.

If this describes your situation, why not try your own bit of aversion therapy by not using cigarettes as your crutch? Learn to assert yourself in different ways. Can you leave your children with a friend one morning a week so you can do what you want to do for a few hours? Or take your kids with you to the swimming pool or out for a picnic with a friend and her children? Can you perhaps think of a hobby or paid job that you can do from home to fit in with your baby or small child's needs? Can you ask a friend over and both do some exercises to a video?

Just to see how much stress you are feeling at the moment, answer the following questions:

1. Do you find it increasingly difficult to get up in the mornings?

2. Do you want to scream at the children for the smallest of misdemeanours – and then feel racked with guilt?

3. Do you feel too tired to cook in the evening?

4. Do you find it difficult to concentrate?

5. Do you often get headaches?

6. Do you suffer from dizzy spells?

7. Have you recently been divorced?

8. Have you recently been made redundant or do you feel you might be soon?

9. Are you having problems paying your mortgage?

10. Have you moved home recently?

11. Has a close member of your family died recently?

12. Are you dreading another Christmas celebration?

If you have answered 'yes' to more than five of the above, you are suffering a great deal of stress and need to take stock.

Quitting smoking is also stressful, so you must try to employ some of the strategies we've talked about. You'll feel much more in control if you manage your stress instead of letting it dictate to you. Once you feel more in control you'll find it much easier to give up smoking for good, become fit and healthy and stay that way.

One of the best coping strategies is to make time for more exercise. Choose something you'll enjoy and **do it regularly** – till it's as much a habit as smoking was.

Get plenty of fresh air – get a dog and exercise it twice a day, buy some flowers (or grow some) and have them about the place and feel happy that you've come this far.

Men and smoking

Men, too, have their crosses to bear. It is not easy for them if they are the sole breadwinner. Who can blame them for putting a cigarette in their mouth at times of extreme pressure? Added to which, some men (and, of course, women) work in smoke-related occupations – just imagine brokers and money markets and people dealing with stocks and shares without smoke pervading. It would be great if they could all decide together not to smoke and try to support each other – once home it is much easier not to light up and I have tried to give lots of suggestions with my aversion strategies. You can't play squash with a cigarette!

Chapter 2

AND NOW ... THE DIET

But in fact, I'm now going to ban the word 'diet' and insert 'healthy/balanced eating' in its place, and I'll tell you why.

To me, the word diet implies suffering and some sort of punishment regime and, more importantly, it implies something fleeting. When you've said, in the past, 'Oh, I must go on a diet,' didn't you mean that you wanted to lose a few kilos/pounds before some special event? Weren't you going on holiday, dating someone new, meeting the prospective in-laws, giving a talk, going to the firm's do, or whatever? And weren't you thinking in terms of a few weeks, or months at the most? Obviously if you start a diet, you finish it, too!

Being obsessed with food is so ridiculous when you think about it – as all of us who have been on a diet know only too well! All that weighing and counting of calories, comparing our weight loss with that of our friends, all the discussions before and after we eat something; all the guilt when we break whatever diet we're following and have a binge, all the recriminations for having done so. All that self-denial and all that guilt and all the precious time invested in *talking* about 'dieting'. It's as if any sort of achievement is out of reach until you're that perfect size 12. Women are notoriously worse than men in their pre-occupation with self-image and that's probably why you see so many men with beer bellies – they think they look fine. Men – read my section on alcohol and beer bellies (pages 50–52)!

Think about it: how many people do you know (and include yourself!) who have tried various diets and are now back to square one – or, dare I say it, even fatter? Their diets may have worked temporarily but what's the point of that?

The best way to achieve your goal is *not* to go on yet another slimming kick but to try to change your way of eating permanently. That means day in and day out. This is what I hope this book will help you achieve. So,

- Don't become neurotic
- Don't become a crank
- Remember: diets definitely don't work
- Eating healthily and exercising works
- Eating a balanced 'diet' works
- And because you'll enjoy this new way of eating, it won't be temporary

A recent study has shown that healthy eating is more economical than it's ever been and that the average employee earns enough money in less than one hour to buy good healthy bread and a carrier-bag full of fruit and vegetables.

Certainly there are lots of cheap and nutritious meals to be made from complex carbohydrates such as bread, potatoes, rice, pasta and cereals. There are lots of pasta and vegetable meals together with bread-based snack ideas further on in the book.

Here's a quiz to see how good or bad your eating habits are:

Test your eating habits

1. Do you get constipated?
2. Are most of your meals tinned or made up from processed foods?
3. Are you hungry an hour after eating?
4. Do you eat fried food every day?

5. Do you seldom eat fish?

6. Is your lunchtime meal made up of junk foods?

7. Do you eat whilst reading or watching TV?

8. Do you eat whilst on the go?

9. Do you add salt before even tasting your food?

10. Do you only eat strawberries with cream and sugar?

11. Do you binge one day and fast the next?

12. Do you eat lots of dairy products?

13. Did you know that drinks and some cereals often contain a lot of sugar?

14. Did you know that fresh fruit and vegetables contain all the natural sugar we need?

15. Do you suffer from high blood pressure?

16. Are you more than 6 kg/14 lbs overweight?

17. Have you tried a new diet within the last year?

18. Do you only eat white bread?

19. Do you always stick to your shopping list or do you buy impulsively?

20. Do you eat between meals?

21. Are you seduced by, say, cream cakes as you pass shop windows?

22. Do you use your car even for short journeys, rather than walk?

23. Do you always use the lift, even for two flights?

24. Do you get out of breath after just one flight?

If you answer 'yes' to more than seven of the above, you are not taking care of yourself, you are not feeding or maintaining your body properly.

Because of the emphasis on healthy and nutritious

food in the quest for a better quality of life, my suggested eating plan is composed of foods thought to be cancer-preventative. Because carcinogens (cancer-causing substances) are found in food as well as tobacco I have avoided any foods suspected of contributing to the development of cancer, e.g. foods which are high in fat, and salted, smoked and pickled foods.

Happily, the foods which may help to prevent cancer, by building up your body's natural defences, are the wholesome and nutritious foods which make up my eating plan. These defensive nutrients and compounds are found in fruits, vegetables and wholegrain cereals.

If you eat fruit, vegetables and wholegrain cereals and pulses you are eating a diet rich in complex carbohydrates and are getting all the necessary nutrients, vitamins, minerals and fibre which you need. This is also such an enjoyable way to eat.

I have based my eating guide on high levels of both fruits and vegetables which contain vitamins and minerals, particularly vitamin C, to protect against heart disease and to give you an extra energy boost for a more active lifestyle.

During this time of tobacco withdrawal, it is vital that your nervous system is well-nourished. This will ensure that:

- you have plenty of energy available

- you have more time for other people's needs, too

- you'll be able to work at top form

It is unnecessary to take any vitamins or minerals in pill form if you follow the suggested eating guide from which you should be able to obtain all the nutrients you need for good health.

The Five Golden Groups of Food

For a 100% healthy way of eating, which should not cause you to put on any weight, I have based my eating plan on foods which are rich in the following nutrients, which I have called the Five Golden Groups.

Vitamin C has a starring role in my plan. It is found in most fruit and vegetables, especially in strawberries, blackcurrants, all citrus fruit, kiwi fruit, melons, tomatoes, peppers, and vegetables such as cabbage and broccoli.

It is extremely helpful when you are withdrawing from tobacco.

- Foods, containing vitamin C protect against heart disease.

- Foods rich in vitamin C give you the extra energy you need to combat withdrawal symptoms.

A new scientific report from the Fresh Fruit and Vegetable Information Bureau (May '92) has shown that men who drink five glasses of orange juice a day may be able to add an extra six years to their lives. Vitamin C can reduce heart attacks by up to 45 per cent in men and up to 25 per cent in women, and just one orange will give you more than $\frac{3}{4}$ of the needed daily requirement of vitamin C.

Beta-carotene is thought to play an important part in the prevention of cancers, heart disease and cataracts. The goodness of beta-carotene cannot be stressed enough. It is recommended that you take 15 mg of beta-carotene daily – which you can easily get from foods such as spinach, tomato, broccoli, greens and, especially, carrots – which have a higher level than any other vegetable. (250 g/8 oz carrots will give you the recommended daily intake of beta-carotene – you will see that I recommend raw carrot sticks as a snack for 'danger times' in my eating plan.)

Selenium (which experimental evidence suggests may possibly prevent cancers, including those of the breast and colon) can be found in tuna, onions and garlic, mushrooms, bran and wheatgerm.

Vitamin E can be found in wholegrain cereals, wheatgerm, soya beans and leafy green vegetables.

Complex carbohydrates (the most nutritious form of carbohydrates) such as bread, cereals, beans and peas.

Try to eat at least three vegetables a day. This should be no hardship because they are delicious and there is such a variety to choose from. Especially beneficial are the vegetables which contain beta-carotene, such as spinach, carrots and broccoli and those containing lots of vitamin C, which include green peppers, cauliflower, broccoli and spring greens. Don't peel your vegetables as you'll lose most of the fibre and nutrients – just scrub them with a vegetable brush.

Eat at least three pieces of fruit each day. This also is no hardship – again there is such a variety around. Amongst the most delicious and beneficial are those containing beta-carotene like apricots, peaches, bananas and cantaloupe melons. Fruits rich in vitamin C, among others, are strawberries, grapefruit, oranges and tangerines. Why not add fruit to your breakfast cereal and give up sugar?

Why eat raw food?

- It's delicious and undeniably better for you than any form of cooked food.
- It's quick and simple to prepare and may reduce your fuel bills too!
- Raw food is more satisfying than cooked.
- Vegetables are much more filling when they are raw.
- It increases your fibre and reduces your cholesterol level.

Carbohydrates

There are two kinds of carbohydrates – simple and complex. They are the source of energy (calories) in our diet. Simple carbohydrates are sugars, contained in sugary drinks and sweets. All they do is add calories, without providing nutrients, and my healthy eating plan does not include sugar.

Complex carbohydrates are the starches found in rice, pasta, bread, cereals, fruit, vegetables and wholegrains. These should make up the bulk of your daily diet. Complex carbohydrates take longer to digest so they keep you feeling full for longer – and therefore less inclined to snack between meals. They are the mainstay of my healthy eating plan.

Sugar

I've got a sweet tooth, how will I cope?

It shouldn't be too difficult for you to cope as *natural* sugar is present in fruit, of which there are so many varieties available in the shops and supermarkets.

- Try eating fruit or sultanas or raisins (in moderation) if you feel the need for something sweet.

- Drink freshly-squeezed juices or low-calorie drinks.

- Don't use sugar in your cooking recipes unless you have to and, even then, use very little – or a liquid sweetener.

- If you use tinned fruit, buy those canned in natural juice.

- If you usually take sugar in your tea and coffee, why not try a substitute sweetener? Best of all, wean yourself off sugar for good.

Watch out for all the different kinds of sugar used in prepared foods: dextrose, fructose, sucrose, glucose and maltose are all sugars. **Read the labels carefully.** These sugars will be listed in the ingredients. Don't be fooled into thinking you are buying sugar-free foods.

Fibre

___

Fibre (also known as bulk or roughage) is found in cereals, wholegrains, nuts, seeds, fruits and vegetables. Fibre is not a nutrient – most types are not digested by the body at all – but it is an extremely valuable part of what you eat.

Fibre works by absorbing water in the intestines (if you need an analogy, think of rice swelling as it absorbs water as it cooks). This increases the bulk of the body's waste products, enabling them to be excreted more efficiently, and generally keeping the system 'regular' and healthy. It is thought that some high-fibre foods (particularly lentils, oats and bran) may be able to reduce the levels of cholesterol in the blood. And studies are now going on to determine whether a high-fibre diet can help to control diabetes.

Quiz No. 2
Are you eating enough fibre?

_____

1. Which of the following is your staple diet for breakfast?
   (a) porridge oats
   (b) high-fibre cereal
   (c) toast, butter and jam
   (d) fry-up, i.e. eggs, bacon, sausages, tomatoes

2. Which type of bread do you regularly eat?
   (a) wholemeal
   (b) brown
   (c) rye
   (d) white

3. How many slices of bread do you eat daily?
   (a) 6 or more
   (b) 4
   (c) 2
   (d) 1 or 2 crispbreads

4. Which of the following snacks would you be likely to eat?
   (a) baked beans on toast
   (b) kidney bean salad
   (c) poached egg on toast
   (d) burger and chips

5. How many of the following do you have each day as part of your main meal? Jacket potato, broccoli, cauliflower, beans, wholegrain rice, tomato, onion, mushroom, cabbage?
   (a) 5 or more
   (b) 4 or 5
   (c) 3
   (d) 1 to 3

6. How many pieces of fruit do you eat each day?
   (a) 5 or more
   (b) 4 or 5
   (c) 3
   (d) 1 to 2

7. Do you have one of the following at each meal daily? Porridge, high-fibre cereal, wholemeal bread, wholemeal pasta or wholegrain rice
   (a) always
   (b) usually
   (c) sometimes
   (d) seldom

How to score:

Score five points for every time you ticked (a)
     four points for every (b)
     three points for every (c)
     one point for every (d)

30–35 – terrific – you certainly seem to eat enough fibre, just ensure you make your meals interesting by ringing the changes and adding touches of colour – i.e. chopped parsley to your pasta and rice dishes, sliced tomatoes to your beans on toast, sliced kiwi fruit to your porridge oats, sweetcorn to your baked potatoes.

21–29 – well done, you're almost there. If you increase your fibre intake by a third you'll not only enjoy your meals more but you'll be improving your health and vitality.

15–20 – you really could do a lot better. Read the section on fibre and see how you can increase your intake daily, feel fuller and less likely to get hunger pangs between meals.

less than 15 – you really don't eat enough fibre and probably feel like snacking all day. Why not try to introduce more fibre-rich foods into every meal, starting with breakfast? You'd be amazed how easy it is and how glad you'll be that you won't succumb to a jam doughnut mid-morning!

You should add more fibre to your diet because high-fibre foods fill you up and leave you feeling full for longer. They are slow-release foods which keep energy levels high so the need to snack between meals is reduced. You should eat a minimum of 30 g/1 oz of fibre a day.

Refining – and why people choose the wrong colour foods!

People tend to choose white products rather than wholemeal (brown) because white flour makes lighter, larger, baked goods which look much better than those made with wholemeal flour. The process of removing the fibre and improving the colour of foods is called refining. Refining removes the husk which is now recognized as containing valuable nutrients and fibre. So remember, when you go shopping, **choose brown!**

One word of warning, however: be moderate in increasing your fibre intake. If you take *too* much it may prevent full absorption of essential nutrients and minerals into your bloodstream. It is better to increase your fibre with fruit and vegetables rather than with bran.

How to *gradually* increase your fibre intake

- Cut your bread (stoneground wholemeal) in thicker slices.

- Choose the wholemeal version of pitta bread.

- Bake with wholemeal flour.

- Eat breakfast cereals with a high fibre content.

- Eat porridge oats – this is one of the best breakfasts you can eat and leaves you feeling full for hours. Make with low-fat milk or half water, half milk.

- Drink plenty of clear fluids as you increase your fibre intake (remember the analogy with rice).

- Eat brown wholegrain rice as a main meal or as a salad.

- Eat wholemeal pasta with low-fat toppings (see recipes).

- Make sure at least one of your meals includes some peas, beans or lentils or make them the meal itself (see recipes).

- If you can't give up nuts as a snack or with a drink, eat them 'natural', unsalted.

- If you miss biscuits and cakes dreadfully, try dried fruits instead, but not too many.

- Eat your potatoes baked, as most of the fibre is just under the skin. They're a meal in itself (see recipe suggestions for fillings which are not fatty).

- Don't peel vegetables such as carrots; scrub with a vegetable brush so as not to strip away any nutrients or fibre.

- Add fruit to your muesli or cereal – no need for any sugar.

You will see that to increase your fibre should not put a burden on the purse-strings – baked, butter, kidney and broad beans, potatoes for baking and home-made muesli are inexpensive but are both nutritious and delicious.

Fats

It is important to know the different kinds of fats – saturated, polyunsaturated and monounsaturated.

Junk foods contain saturated fat – foods like burgers and hot dogs, also meat and anything made from it, like beef, pork, lamb, sausages, luncheon meats, ribs, brisket, corned beef. It is also prevalent in dairy products, not skimmed milk but in half-cream and full-cream milk and cream, in butter and full-fat yogurts, soft cheeses, ice-cream (but not the lower-fat type), cheese dips, cheese spreads, custard (made with full or half-cream milk), condensed, evaporated and dried milk. It is also found in duck, goose and chicken skin and it is for this reason that you are always advised to eat your chicken skinless. You need to read the contents on the label when you buy oil because not all vegetable oils are good for you. Watch out for palm oil and coconut oil which are high in saturated fat. Cakes, biscuits, cooking fats and hard margarine are all high in saturated fats. Also pancakes, waffles, cocoa butter, puddings and sauces in general.

Saturated fat is the fat which tends to produce cholesterol. This can build up on the walls of the arteries which supply blood to the heart, causing them to narrow over the years and eventually become blocked, causing heart disease. One of the ways you can help reduce your risk is not to eat saturated fat which is found in red meat, especially offal, dairy produce and eggs, palm and coconut oils. Instead, eat foods containing **polyunsaturated fats**: margarines and oils made from soya, corn, sunflower and grapeseed. Also eat foods containing the omega 3 fatty acids which are thought to help lower blood fats, reducing the risk of formation of blood clots which cause fatal heart attacks. This is a very important fact for smokers, who produce a protein called fibrinogen which produces blood clots. The omega 3 fatty acids play a vital role in making the platelets in our blood less sticky and making the arteries less vulnerable to hardening.

These fatty acids are found in fish oil and oily fish such as mackerel, herring and salmon and form a very important part of my eating guide. You should eat these fish at least twice a week.

Monounsaturated fats. These, like polyunsaturated oil, are found primarily in plants and are also liquid at room temperature (whereas saturated fats are solid). Sources of monounsaturated fats are olive oil, avocados and peanuts. Olive oil is considered to be very healthy for your heart and is said to reduce the risk of a heart attack.

How difficult will it be to change from foods containing saturated to unsaturated fats?

It will be very easy indeed. Here are just a few changes you can make:

- Drink skimmed or semi-skimmed milk instead of full-fat. (If you use the low-fat milk which I suggest, which is calcium-enriched, you won't detect any difference in taste.)

- Buy a low-fat spread which is low in saturates, such as olive-oil spread. Don't eat butter or other margarines unless they are high in polyunsaturates.

- Don't eat cream or half-cream.

- Change to low-fat cheeses: Edam, Gouda or cottage cheese, and cheese spreads which are made with polyunsaturated oils. Also low-fat curd cheese, and fromage frais which is excellent as:
    a filling for jacket potatoes, with some chopped chives
    a dessert topping instead of cream
    a dip, mixed with herbs
    in casseroles
    sauce for chicken, mixed with watercress
    in soup, instead of a dollop of cream

- Try not to fry your food – grill, steam, bake or boil instead. If you do fry, try stir-frying in a wok which will need very little oil (remember to make it a polyunsaturated oil). Or use a non-stick pan.

- Cut all fat off meat before cooking and remember that most of the fat in poultry is just under the skin – so if you skin your chicken before cooking you'll have no problems.
- Concentrate on eating fish and poultry – never burgers, sausages or pies, unless you are making them yourself, in which case you would use low-fat fillings.
- If you like to add a dash of cream to your soup, try fromage frais instead.
- Casserole your meat instead of roasting.

If you are worried about heart attacks ...

- Eat oily fish at least twice a week. This should be enjoyable and easy as there are quite a number of fatty fish to choose from – mackerel, herrings, sardines, tuna, salmon, mullet, halibut, hake, sea bass, plaice, haddock and shellfish.

- Work out your daily intake so that you really enjoy what you are eating (there are hints to help you do that later in the book).

- Eat more fibre.

- Eat less sugar – if you eat too much it raises fat levels in your blood.

- Cut down drastically on your salt intake.

- Drink alcohol in moderation (see pages 50–53) but don't deprive yourself – you're aiming to be happy.

- Eat foods rich in polyunsaturates which reduce the amount of cholesterol in the blood and help prevent heart disease.

Junk foods – and why they won't do

You know what we mean by junk foods – the soggy hamburgers with chips, fatty sausages, pork pies, fried snacks like crisps, biscuits and cakes – all of which contain a lot of fat and leave you feeling hungry quite a short while after eating them.

There is a difference, of course, if you have a 100% lean meat hamburger served with crunchy raw vegetables and a wholemeal bun. Also don't confuse convenience foods like frozen vegetables and frozen fish – which are, of course, good for you – with junk.

It's easy to pick junk foods because you're starving and can't wait to reach home and a properly-balanced meal. Resist the temptation; you *can* wait.

A plate of steak and kidney pudding with chips, followed by apple crumble and custard or sherry trifle will look and smell tempting. But, even if you are slim on the outside, when you eat so much fat in one meal, the fat goes into your stomach and gets absorbed into the bloodstream which circulates it round the body and, over a number of years, cholesterol and fat are gradually deposited in the lining of the arteries, making them narrower. The result is that the heart has to pump harder; the blood pressure goes up just to get the blood through and the heart is put under strain, and you risk a heart attack.

The good news is that the effects are reversible if you can change the way you eat. But remember it all boils down to **being prepared**. Buy the right food in the supermarket and have it ready to hand, so you don't fall into temptation.

Some other important nutrients

Iron
This important nutrient is found in fortified breakfast cereals, as well as in liver and red meat. It is also found in

pulses and vegetables such as lentils, in baked beans, kidney beans and haricot, in spinach and also in fish.

Calcium

This is vital for healthy bones and teeth. It will also help to ease the stress you are under while giving up smoking. As my eating plan is low in dairy foods (the most common source of calcium) I use a calcium-enriched, low-fat milk. Other good sources are nuts, pulses and broccoli.

Vitamin B

This is found in wholemeal and wholewheat flour, yeast extract, brewer's yeast and pulses. This vitamin will keep you from becoming despondent and will calm your nerves.

Now that we've looked at the basic building blocks of my eating plan, we can look at putting it into practice.

How to eat healthily

Healthy eating is not a matter of diet but a matter of balance. Look after the pennies and you'll look after the pounds might well apply to this matter of balance. If you get your complex carbohydrates right and don't eat any of the wrong type of fat, the calories will be balanced too.

This is what stops junk foods being OK to eat. If you fill yourself up with junk foods, which are full of fat and sugar, you will have little room to eat the proper balance of vegetables, pulses, fruits and bread/pasta which you need and which you'll enjoy.

Balance your fat, fibre and natural sugar

The calories will take care of themselves

Start in the supermarket – that's where it all begins

You can't eat the wrong things if you've only stocked up your larder with the right ones.

Here's a list of reminders:

- Only shop with a list – then you won't be seduced into impulse buying of the 'wrong' foods.

- Choose poultry – not fatty meat – and remember to remove the skin before cooking.

- Choose fatty fish (and eat it at least twice a week).

- Buy tins of tuna, sardines, mackerel, pilchards, packed in water or brine – you will be getting sufficient oil in the rest of your diet. Eat the bones which are full of calcium.

- Buy very low-fat milk enriched with calcium.

- Buy polyunsaturated low-fat spreads – e.g. made from olive oil.

- Buy lowest fat hard cheeses, e.g. Edam and Gouda.

- Buy lowest fat soft cheeses – cottage, fromage frais and quark.

- Buy Camembert and Brie which are semi-fat.

- Buy low-fat natural yogurt – add chopped fruit at home.

- Buy ingredients to make up home-made soups, salads; don't buy ready-made versions.

- Remember ingredients for fresh fruit desserts, non-fattening sauces for pasta.

- Wholemeal bread.

- Wholegrain vitamin-enriched cereals.

- Wholegrain rice.

- Porridge oats.

- Peas, beans and lentils – can be meals in themselves.

Now you have a range of polyunsaturated foods which look after the fat levels (cholesterol) in your blood.

You have foods containing vitamin C which we have said you need for extra energy whilst giving up smoking.

You have foods containing calcium which will help ease the stress you are under whilst giving up smoking and will help retain mobility in your joints as you get older.

And you have foods containing vitamin B which will keep you from becoming too despondent and calm your nerves.

Chapter 3

THE FIRST DAY OF THE REST OF YOUR LIFE

The key thing is to **be prepared**. During the day there are bound to be **danger times**, when you either crave a cigarette, or you long for a chocolate bar. You are bound to suffer from these to some degree. So here is advanced warning of some likely temptations, and some strategies for dealing with them.

When you first wake up. If you were one of those people who immediately puts a cigarette in their mouth on waking, take your mind off it by starting the day with either a swim, walking the dog or turning on the exercise video. I plumped for swimming which is wonderfully soothing and refreshing and really sets you up for the day – you'll find you have boundless energy after a swim. Start off gradually with perhaps two or three lengths, till you can comfortably manage 10 or 12 without being breathless. It gets easier each time – just as each day becomes easier without a cigarette. You'll find you really look forward to your swim and maybe even jump out of bed raring to go. Have at least two swimsuits so you don't spend ages locating a dry one, and have your sports bag packed and ready the night before. You can also shower and shampoo your hair at the swimming pool and go straight on to work or go home for breakfast.

Breakfast time should not be too much of a danger time as most people are dashing to catch their train or bus. Remember to have a proper breakfast of slow-release foods which will keep you going till lunchtime.

Your breakfast should comprise: fruit juice or piece of fruit, high-fibre cereals or oatmeal porridge (you can add your piece of fruit to either) or home-made muesli made with fruit, coffee or tea with milk or a natural low-fat yogurt (which you can chop that piece of fruit into).

Don't forget to take your packed lunch to work with you.

Coffee time at the office is the next danger time, when perhaps the office trolley laden with doughnuts, crisps and rolls arrives. Get into the habit of not even looking at the array. Once you have got used to having your healthy eating breakfast you shouldn't be hungry but, if you are, bring out a piece of fruit that you packed the night before, or pack a couple of carrots (don't peel them as all the goodness is under the skin).

Lunchtime may prove difficult for some of you who have been used to going to the pub for a couple of drinks and a pie. The strategy here is to eat two-thirds of your packed lunch which will be either a stoneground wholemeal sandwich or pitta bread filled with one of the recipe suggestions on pages 109–112, or some made-up salads that you've brought in plastic containers. In the winter you can bring some home-made soups in a thermos, wholemeal roll, salad and two pieces of fruit. You'll feel much better if you eat your lunch and go for a walk. If there's a pool or exercise class near your work, why not go there, returning afterwards to eat your lunch? Have a browse round a museum or art gallery if you're near one. Maybe there are some antique shops or a market nearby that would be interesting to explore, and a brisk walk there and back would be energizing. How about a walk to a pretty square where you can take a book and relax for a while? Certainly you'll feel more invigorated and ready to tackle the afternoon after a light but filling lunch and a short bout of exercise. When you used to succumb to a junk-ridden burger and chips at lunchtime,

I bet you felt lethargic all afternoon. If you used to just grab a packet of crisps and a chocolate bar, no doubt you were ravenous by the time you left the office and bought yet another 'junk' snack to see you home.

Be prepared

Each night, before going to bed, get ready a plastic container filled with carrot sticks and/or celery and eat the contents when you're feeling hungry between breakfast and lunch – perhaps when the doughnut-laden trolley comes around!

For lots of people there is a danger time at about **4 o'clock**. If you are at home with children, you may have picked them up from school and given them tea and it's too soon yet to put on the dinner and you want or need to eat. What I suggest to you, in this case, is to eat the balance of your lunch. So if you were making a wholemeal sandwich for your lunch that day, make $1\frac{1}{2}$ sandwiches (i.e. use 3 pieces of bread). Eat one for lunch and the remaining half at the time when you're absolutely dying for a cigarette or, now that you've given up, some food to take its place. Think of this extra half a sandwich as your saviour because that's just what it is. It certainly won't do you any harm

- there's plenty of time to work it off

- it will stave off any cravings to buy any junk to fill the void

- it'll leave you with much more energy

- best of all you won't be feeling deprived, wanting to chuck it all in and have a cigarette

- you won't feel you've blown it

- so you'll continue not smoking but eating well for yet another day.

I found that after I'd managed three days of living like this, without a cigarette, I didn't want to ruin it all by starting smoking again because the first three days were *not* easy. I did want to eat in place of smoking a cigarette, and eating between 40 and 50 times a day was ludicrous! But at least eating 40 carrot sticks is preferable to 40 packets of crisps or sweets, and each day you'll find you need that much less.

For office workers, however, the dangertime is probably **5:00/5:30ish** when perhaps colleagues are going on to a wine bar to have a drink and chat for an hour or so, before travelling for another hour or so, and perhaps not reaching home and sitting down to eat properly until way past 8 o'clock. The trick here is to have your remaining sandwich just before you leave the office, with perhaps an apple or banana. In this way

- you won't be tempted to scoff the peanuts at the wine bar

- you won't drink too much because
  a) either you're fed up not being able to smoke
  b) or to fill yourself up because you're hungry
  c) or you'll think it's hours till you get home to eat and you need a lift

- you won't eat a snack from the kiosk at the station whilst you wait for your evening train

- you'll have much more energy left for your evening at home

- your journey won't feel so tiring

- you'll be able to concentrate on a book on the way home

- you won't have blown it, or feel discouraged and so give up . . .

A danger time for all of us surely is **after dinner** particularly at a restaurant or after a specially delicious meal. That is one of the most difficult habits to break because you associate the cigarette as the final part of the meal. It's very difficult to find a solution to this one other than not to dine out with friends who smoke; the cigarette smoke wafting in your nostrils from their cigarettes is almost too much to bear. After you've kicked the habit, this tempting feeling becomes less and less, so it's a good idea to avoid your smoking friends just for the initial couple of weeks. Once you've given up you will find that other people's smoke in restaurants is an abomination and wonder how you could ever have smoked!

Inevitably, **parties** are danger times when everyone is eating, drinking and smoking. I think the way out of this is to have each of your hands occupied, the whole time. In other words, have a glass in one hand and a plate in the other. The glass could contain mineral water or fruit juice or it could contain champagne, spirits or wine (but try to make it last all evening if it does). If you're used to having a drink to unwind, as you get in from work, don't give it up – but either:

a) have one now and one with your dinner (see safe alcohol levels, pages 50–52)

   or

b) try one from the recipes at the back of the book – for example a tomato juice with tabasco and plenty of ice or home-made mango juice.

Remember this is not a 'do without' way of living, it's a 'try this instead' way of living – without giving up any enjoyment.

Most people's worst time is **the evening** – that's the time to take up a sport or a hobby and not just slump in front of the TV which will inevitably lead to thinking about snacking especially when the programmes are boring . . .

If **lazy Sundays at home** are your problem, don't let them take the form of any laziness which associates itself in your mind with smoking. You might want to take up a sport instead, learning to sail or horse ride, take a bicycle out for the day, each weekend, have friends over for a picnic, take your children/grandchildren to the park and help them fly a kite or feed the deer, play a game of ball in your back yard – there really are umpteen things you can do.

If **holidays** are your problem and you've been working hard all year, longing for this two-week break in the sun and you've been used to having a smoke on the beach or round the pool, why not try a different type of holiday this year – one that does not become associated in your mind with smoking as a means of relaxing. Try an activity holiday – there are so many you'll be spoilt for choice: pony trekking, walking, painting and so on. Alternatively, holiday in towns, so you can't just lie on the beach – looking at art galleries in Florence for example. Why not combine a beach/activity holiday in one? If you can manage your usual holiday without feeling you have to smoke, good luck. It's only the first few weeks that will be difficult.

Answering the telephone. This is a hard one for a lot of people. If you're at home, put one of those novelties next to the phone and play with that. At the office, fiddle with some worry beads, doodle or draw.

Studying. Whilst you're studying, perhaps for an exam or doing your evening class homework, it will be quite hard to begin with, especially if your studying lasts for a long time. Maybe one of the following suggestions might help:

- Have a bowl of crudités at your side – raw carrot, celery, sprigs of raw cauliflower etc. – to nibble when you might before have lit up a cigarette.

- Have a jug of mineral water and a glass with slices of fresh lemon in, to refresh you.

- Don't study for too long. Break up your studying time by going out for a walk to get some fresh air.

There are unfortunately always times when you will feel tempted at first to reach for a cigarette or a snack

- when you're relaxing

- when you're bored

- when there are crises to be faced

- when you're socializing

- when you are at a business lunch.

The mood will pass and the good news is that this 'suffering' will not last long. Don't give in to it – it'll just lengthen the process and it'll make you feel discouraged.

Here are a few tips to encourage you when you feel the urge to smoke or eat cream cakes:

1. Think: Do I need it?

2. Keep thinking how tremendously difficult it was to give up in the first place. Do you really want all that pain again? The moment will pass and boy will you feel great!

3. Get out your holiday brochures!

4. Go for a swim.

5. Mend a shelf or wash your hair, give yourself a face pack or paint your nails.

6. Chew sugar-free gum – this really helps – but not on an empty stomach.

Take it just one day at a time. Each morning, when you wake up and realize that you haven't 'blown it' and that you've achieved yet another day, will give you greater impetus to continue. Before long a week has passed, then a month, six months and you'll realize that you've swapped one or two bad habit(s) for GREAT ONES!

Home/office help

If you can't bear the thought of making your own sandwiches the night before and covering them in cling-film ready to take out of the fridge next morning, then buy them, remembering the following points:

- Choose wholemeal sandwiches filled with fish, cottage cheese and salad. Don't buy white bread with fatty fillings like cheese or meat or anything laden with mayonnaise.

- Buy fruit instead of a pudding.

- Buy Diet Coke or mineral water, not squashes that are full of sugar.

- Buy low-fat natural yogurt not the fruit yogurt with sugar.

- Buy fruit if you don't manage to bring your carrot with you!

In other words don't choose processed or refined foods – you won't feel nearly so satisfied and you'll feel hungry more quickly, too.

Some practical tactics for home

- When you feel like eating something more, clean your teeth – it really works.

- Try to keep occupied in the evening – this is really the time to take up a hobby or sport you enjoy or to go for a walk. If you've decided to stay in why not tackle a jigsaw? They are fun and will keep your hands busy.

- Don't invite people in who smoke – not till you're confident it won't bother you.

- Why not take up an art class, or an evening class or correspondence course?

Tips

★ Don't go shopping when you're hungry.

★ Give yourself lots of chewy food, like crunchy vegetables. If you chew, you don't eat so fast and so you'll feel more satisfied at the end.

★ Don't eat standing up or on the go because you'll feel you haven't eaten.

★ If you used to smoke when watching TV, then read a book instead or go to an evening class.

★ Give yourself a manicure instead of smoking – at least you'll have beautiful nails (if you haven't bitten them all off in frustration).

★ If you are going out to eat in a restaurant, phone in advance if you want them to prepare something for you that fits in with your healthy eating.

★ Don't use salt substitute – it's more harmful than salt! Use herbs in place of salt.

★ Cutting out a meal will not make you slim.

★ Chart the troublesome times and find coping strategies – either do your 20 minutes of exercise or start your hobby or study session.

★ Don't have second helpings – ever.

★ Kick-start your campaign to give up smoking and eat well without putting on weight by a visit to the hygienist – it's amazing what a good start this gives you – you won't want to ruin your clean teeth and breath with a foul-smelling cigarette!

★ Tell everyone you're stopping smoking but don't mention a word about trying to maintain your weight so that your efforts stand a good chance of not being sabotaged!

★ When someone offers you a cigarette, just say 'no thank you, I've given up!'

★ If you've a real craving for something sweet, eat some raisins. The energy you get from raisins comes from fruit sugars. They contain virtually no fat at all, they contain iron and are high in fibre – add them to your cereal, to your rice dishes and your salads – you can soak them overnight to make them fatter. Always have them in stock.

Special situations

_____

Eating out

_____

Whether it's a business lunch, a dinner party or a private celebration, the key thing is to **be prepared**.

First of all, your object is to enjoy life, and if you're eating healthy well-balanced meals **90%** of the time, it really doesn't matter if you deviate for the remaining 10%. However, if the thought of doing so worries you, and you'd rather not deviate even once, then plan ahead. But don't refuse an invitation whatever you do; don't spoil your life for the sake of your diet; the diet must fit in with your life.

When you know you're going out and will eat more than usual, or you may be unable to have the food you normally eat as part of your healthy eating plan, then go easy and eat less for the preceding day or two – it makes sense and you'll feel good about things the day after the outing. Remember we have never had it so good with hoteliers and restaurateurs offering healthy alternative menus but here is a guide to help you choose what to eat:

Choose:

- chicken (you can always remove the skin yourself)

- liver which is full of iron. Ask for it to be grilled not fried

- fish, but not with a rich sauce – it's just as enjoyable grilled

- vegetables, especially if they're raw

- melon or grapefruit as a starter, or seafood salad, oysters, *moules marinières*, mushrooms à la grecque, asparagus or home-made soup (without cream)

- fresh fruit salad as dessert or a slice of fresh pineapple, mango, strawberries and raspberries – delicious and refreshing too

- a tomato juice as your cocktail and a glass of wine mixed with mineral water with your meal. Don't let people keep filling your glass when you've only drunk part – you'll never keep count of how much you've drunk

- if you're having salad, ask for the dressing on the side and just add as much as you need.

Avoid:

- creamy soups and starters in pastry – they'll be full of fat

- pâtés, fatty meats, vegetables cooked in cheese sauces and chips. Have a jacket or boiled new potatoes instead

- creamy, sugar-laden desserts. You'll feel much better if you pass them by

- don't be tempted to eat your roll and butter whilst waiting for your first course.

Tips for eating out

- Remember to eat **slowly**.

- Put small amounts of food on your fork.

- Listen to the conversation and join in – that should slow you down.

- Don't have second helpings, however much your hosts insist.

- You do not have to eat everything on your plate.

- Be moderate – with careful thought beforehand and good selection at the time, you can have a marvellous meal and not feel deprived.

Ethnic restaurants should not pose problems. In Chinese restaurants, choose dishes that are steamed or stir-fried.

There are lots of fish and chicken dishes and with rice and vegetables you'll be fine. With Indian restaurants try tandoori dishes; with salad and rice or vegetables there is plenty of choice.

Christmas/Thanksgiving

It is always a great temptation at Christmas or Thanksgiving to say 'I'll eat everything, it's only once a year.' I don't think it's worth it to stuff yourself full of turkey, sweet potatoes, pumpkin pie, Christmas pudding and brandy butter and indulge in the truffles and endless chocolates and mince pies at *every* meal. There are lots of occasions that happen only once a year!

Why not have turkey (without the skin) and an exotic fruit salad for dessert? If you feel you really don't want to deprive yourself of the traditional fare, **be prepared** and cut down for a few days before. In that way you can indulge a bit and not feel guilty about it afterwards.

Foreign holidays: what to eat and what to avoid when travelling abroad

Australia
Australians are renowned for eating chops and two veg every night. Although Australia has wonderful meat, especially beef, do try to eat seafood instead and a great variety of vegetables and fruit. Avoid traditional pastries and meat pies – on every lunchtime menu!

Austria
Do avoid famous dishes like wiener schnitzel and boiled beef with knodel (dumplings), the sausages and rich chocolate cake. Don't forget nearly everything comes with cream, e.g. apfelstrudel.

Belgium
Eat the mussels and chicken stews, but avoid sausages and pâté, rich in pork fat. Steer clear of waffles.

The Caribbean
Avoid sugar cakes, coconut drops, pineapple fudge, banana cookies and shave ice (West Indians do have a very sweet tooth). Eat rotis (chapatis filled with curry), yams, christophene (vegetable like a marrow), callaloo (like spinach), green bananas, avocados (sometimes called alligator pear or midshipman's butter), aubergine, salmon (known as weak fish or bangomaree), pineapples, pomegranate, mango, paw paw, granadilla. Fish is plentiful and there's a good variety: choose from flying fish, red snapper, barracuda. Don't forget you can get brown rice and black-eyed peas, red beans and chick peas, all excellent sources of vegetarian protein.

Denmark
Be wary of all dairy foods and Danish pastries, also bread and beer soup (porridge) – try open sandwiches instead.

France
Avoid all the rich pâtés, terrines and mousses – go instead for crudités and salads, buy wholemeal bread instead of the ubiquitous white baguette (there are wholemeal versions). Choose from a wide variety of fish and seafood and omit the rich creamy sauced dishes. Avoid (if you can – or limit yourself vigorously): *pain au chocolat* and croissants and the wonderful *tartes*. Avoid egg and potato dishes in cream. Eat plenty of vegetables, and fruit for dessert.

Germany
Try to avoid sausages, salamis and pork dishes, as well as potato pancakes and doughnuts!

Greece
Avoid the sweet pastries like baklava, go easy on the Moussaka and cheese-filled pastries, omit the ouzo! There are lots of lovely kebabs, chicken and fish, plenty of salads and fruits.

India

Try to avoid the dishes made with cream – and go for lentil dishes (called dal) which are a wonderful source of vegetarian protein. Avoid bhajis (deep-fried vegetables in batter). There is plenty of fish (e.g. hilsa (a river and sea fish, like salmon), pomfret, koimarch, and magurmarch) and rice. Go for nan bread which is baked in a clay oven rather than parathas which are fried. Chapatis are cooked over a *tava* (an inverted pan) and held with tongs over an open fire. Fruit in India can be delicious and there is a wide range from which to choose: custard apples, guavas, mangos, water melons, jack fruits, pomegranates, chikus and bananas. There is an equally impressive range of vegetables, including okra, brinjal (aubergine), parbal (baby cucumbers), peppers (red, green, purple), beans, carrots and potatoes. There is lots of dried fruit to munch instead of sweets and chocolates: prunes, figs, dates, raisins, plums, apricots. Avoid coconuts (saturated fat).

Israel

Avoid lockshen pudding (pudding made from egg noodles, eggs, sugar, margarine, dried fruit and spices), cholent (beef casserole), kugel, traditional gefilte fish – if fried (they can be boiled, too). Also potato latkes (potato pancakes), apple strudel and honey cake. Israel grows an abundance of fruit and vegetables. Try the sharon fruits, oranges from the citrus groves all around the country and avocado pears. Wonderful choice of melons, chicken and fish.

Italy

Eat the pasta, gnocchi, and risotto, the wonderful vegetable omelettes, the fresh sardines, whitebait, swordfish, scampi and squid. Avoid (if you possibly, possibly can) the rich creamy pasta sauces – go for fresh Neapolitan tomato sauce, made from tomatoes, onions with parsley and chives. Restrict your ice-creams, too.

Spain

Go for paella – don't have everything swimming in oil.

Switzerland
The Swiss do have a way with potatoes – try to avoid them!
Also their wonderful patisserie, and chocolate.

Turkey
Eat the cucumber in yogurt with garlic and the stuffed
peppers. Avoid the thick, very sweet coffee and the filo
pastry stuffed with cheese.

Drinking

You need to cut down if you usually drink

- more than 21 units a week (men)

- more than 14 units a week (women)

You are on the way to addiction if you usually drink

- 28 units a week (men)

- 20 units a week (women)

one unit = one single shot of spirits, one standard size glass
of wine or half a pint of beer. Drinking levels are measured
in these units.

A report published in May 1992 by Professor
Gerry Shaper, a public health specialist, finds
that middle-aged men run the risk of 'holiday
heart' – the potentially fatal effect of suddenly
raising the alcohol intake in the relaxing surroundings of sun, sea and sand. And men who
drink more than three pints of beer a day are
twice as likely to drop dead from a sudden
massive heart attack. Prof. Shaper, who led the
study of the health and drinking habits of
thousands of British men, said alcohol raises
blood pressure and causes irregularities of heart
beat which can kill in minutes.

There is a danger in combining alcohol and cigarettes. The risks of getting certain cancers seem to be increased by the effect of the two together.

It may be that you've decided to give wine bars and pubs a miss but, in case you still socialize there, here are a few tips to make things a bit easier for you in your quest for a better quality of life and the cutting-back on your alcohol too.

If you feel the need to make excuses for not drinking as much as you used to, why not try the following gambits:

- I've brought the car today and I obviously can't drink and drive.

- My doctor won't let me drink while I'm taking these tablets.

- I've changed my religion to one which forbids drinking.

- There's something wrong with my throat and drink irritates it.

If none of the above ploys work, here's how to cope:

- When it's your turn to buy a round, buy yourself an orange juice; if you must save face you can pretend it is a vodka and orange. Similarly, a tonic water will easily pass for a gin and tonic, or a ginger ale on its own for whisky with ginger ale.

- Why not drink a spritzer – very popular – half wine and half soda water.

- Try a glass of mineral water with ice and lemon.

- Make sure you only order singles.

- Have a tomato juice.

- Most bars and pubs will have diet drinks which, with ice and lemon, are very refreshing.

Business lunches and dinners may put most strain on your resolve, when drinking seems to go hand in hand with making deals. Just say you don't drink much and leave it at that – it's more fashionable now to have just one glass of wine and drink mineral waters throughout your meal, or omit the wine altogether. You'll find your brain will stay clearer that way, too! It really is much more *à la mode* to be aware of your health now than it ever was before and people do really want to be moderate and enjoy a better quality of life.

Alcohol and fat

When you drink alcohol you burn up fat more slowly. Any fat that isn't burned is stored on the belly, on the thighs and anywhere else that people tend to put on weight. It is not just the calories in alcohol which makes alcohol fattening, it's the way alcohol alters the body's normal way of dealing with fat in the diet.

The body is pretty stingy about the amount of fat it will burn off anyway. When you add extra carbohydrates (sugar or starch) to your diet, the body tends to burn most of it, laying little down as fat, but the body burns extra fat sparingly and tends to store it away.

It is not clear why alcohol slows down fat metabolism but what is clear is what can be done about it – **eat less fat**.

Men and beer bellies

Not everyone who drinks gets a beer belly; beer-guzzlers and whisky-drinkers who live on burgers and crisps certainly will put on weight, but a vegetarian who has the odd glass of white wine will not. Alcohol in itself increases the tick-over speed of the body so you burn off calories more quickly. So if you substitute some of that fatty food for a glass or two of white wine in the evening, the chances are that you'll increase your ability to diet *and* lose a bit of weight.

Having people in for drinks

If you are used to having something to nibble with your drink in the evening before dinner or you've invited in some friends, you might like to serve crudités with a fromage frais dressing – add chives and lemon juice. There are lots of raw vegetables to choose from besides cauliflower sprigs, carrot sticks and radishes. Why not also try some of the following?

Celery, stuffed with curd cheese and sprinkled with paprika, spring onions – leave on their long stems, fennel bulb or coarsely-grated kohlrabi, tomatoes cut into quarters, mange-tout, stoned olives, green, red and yellow peppers cut into strips, stoned fresh dates, broccoli florets.

You'll find most people really do prefer a healthy alternative to the salted crisps or nuts which they're sorry they filled up on.

Chapter 4

EXERCISE – DO I HAVE TO?

═══════════════

I'm not suggesting that you get up at dawn and do press-ups till you drop, but here are some of the benefits you'll get from exercise.

Exercise gives you more vitality; it aids your circulation and therefore your skin; the heart becomes stronger as a result of you working it – which means it can pump more blood round the body. It beats more slowly, arteries open up and your blood pressure lowers. Exercise is enjoyable; like smoking, it relieves tension and, best of all, exercise suppresses the appetite!

- Exercise releases hormones into the bloodstream which help you to feel happier and lift your spirits.

- Exercise helps you sleep.

- It builds strength and stamina.

- It stops your bones becoming brittle.

- It allows you to focus on what you're doing and clears your mind.

- It alleviates headaches.

- It keeps you supple.

- It delays ageing, as your muscles and joints are kept regularly in use.

- It allows you to perform better under duress - i.e. running to the post office before it shuts.

- As you become used to doing exercise on a regular basis you can do more each time and for longer, without becoming breathless into the bargain.

- If the weather is really terrible buy or rent an exercise video to follow at home.

- The more you exercise, the more physical activities you can take part in.

- Because exercise is so good for your circulation, your skin tone and colour should improve.

- You don't need to buy expensive equipment to go to the gym or for a swim.

- Your metabolic rate is buoyant if you exercise.

Why not exercise instead of smoke?

Why not exercise instead of eating snacks?

Exercise need only take 20 minutes, three times a week. That is all you need to do to keep fit. But exercise is like a drug which is habit-forming - you won't want to stop doing it and you'll miss it if you do.

Improve the quality of your life. Exercise together as a family; walk in the park, cycle, jog walk, play.

Set yourself targets you can easily reach. Try to get outdoors as much as you possibly can. You'll be visiting the doctor less frequently; it'll be goodbye to angina and bronchitis and lots of other ailments, too. Why not buy an exercise bike and cycle away whilst watching TV? Whatever you choose to do, you must enjoy it otherwise you won't keep at it long enough to benefit from the fitness and sense of wellbeing it will bring.

Quiz No. 3

Here's a quiz to see if you are fit.

1. Can you walk up two flights of 12 stairs and not be breathless?

2. Can you hold a conversation at the same time?

3. Do you end an aerobic session
   (a) on your knees?
   (b) full of vim and vigour?

4. How well do you sleep:
   (a) very well every night?
   (b) very well from time to time?
   (c) very badly?

5. Do you feel your age?

6. Are you exhausted at the end of the day?

7. Can you walk three or four bus stops without hopping on one?

8. Are you more than 9.5 kg/21 lbs overweight?

9. Do you get easily breathless?

10. Can you keep up with your children when, say, playing in the garden?

Answers:

Score 5 points if you answered 'yes' to questions 1, 2, 3b, 4a, 7 and 10

Score 3 points if you answered 'yes' to question 4b

Score 0 if you answered 'yes' to questions 3a, 4c, 5, 8 and 9

What these scores mean:

Top score possible: 30. If you scored this, excellent. You're just too good to be true.

If you scored between 20 and 25, well done! You do seem to

have grasped the benefits of exercise. To increase your stamina, why not

● walk upstairs every time

● make sure you take your aerobic exercise *three* times weekly, for at least 20 minutes

● leave your car at home except when you are going shopping for heavy groceries

● make sure you maintain your weight

If you scored 10 to 20 points, you really could be much fitter. Read the chapter on exercise and try to understand that the changes in both your exercising and eating patterns need not be major. Try

● walking a few stops on each bus trip you take

● going for a swim three times a week, for 20 minutes.

You'll soon feel fitter and will enjoy doing more each day.

Less than 10 points. It's not as hard as you think. Do give it a try. On the plus side – you obviously want to improve your eating and exercise habits or you wouldn't be reading this book. Good luck! Start today and you'll be pleased you did.

Excuses people make for not exercising

● I can't find the time

No? How long does it take to get off the bus one stop earlier than your destination and walk the rest of the way?

Why can't you go for a brisk walk:

a) in your lunch-hour?
b) on the way to work?
c) after work?
d) on the way to the wine-bar?

If you've got a child or a dog it should be easy and fun.

- I haven't done any exercise for a long time and am worried I'll overdo it.

a) If you are over forty, before doing any exercise more strenuous than a gentle stroll, swim or cycle, check with your doctor.

b) When you're exercising, **stop** the minute you feel any pain – it's not meant to **hurt**.

c) Don't exercise with nimble twelve-year-olds.

d) Build up your stamina **gradually**.

- I feel too exhausted at the end of the day to think of anything other than slumping in front of the television with a drink.

Exercise is the answer for you – it's just the thing that will refresh you and leave you feeling tension-free. You'll sleep better too.

Try one of the following ways

Go for a walk – and make it interesting. Try a different route each day and notice your surroundings. Look at the architecture of the buildings, enjoy the flowers. Make each walk slightly brisker and slightly longer. Walk to the park, notice the progress of the shrubs, the trees, the flowers. Listen to the band. Why not borrow a dog (and let it take you for a walk) – or even buy one with all that money you've saved now that you don't smoke?
    Remember:

- Dress appropriately for walking.

- Trainers or comfortable shoes are a must.

- Walk facing oncoming traffic.

- Wear reflective clothing if walking at night.

- Walk where the street lighting is good.

If you enjoy walking, how about taking up golf? There's certainly a *lot* of walking.

Go for a swim. It's invigorating to go first thing in the morning, a boost at lunchtime and a wind-down in the evening. It really is the best all-round exercise there is, using every muscle gently, with the water cushioning you. You can, of course, make it as energetic as you like.

Another good exercise where you are supported is **cycling**. In the summer months, why not cycle to your nearest beauty spot and have a drink with a friend once you arrive? Use your bike to cycle to the shops, to see friends, or to go to work.

Take up a sport – try tennis, badminton or squash, which are fun and sociable as well as being good for you.

If you don't cycle to work, use public transport, get off the bus one or two stops before your destination, and walk the rest. If you use the underground why not walk up the escalators? Use stairs wherever you can; it's marvellous exercise. Graduate to taking two at a time. Leave your car outside your home and only take it when you've heavy shopping to collect.

If you don't work, or you're retired, set yourself an errand each day which necessitates a walk, be it to post a letter, buy a loaf of bread or collect your evening newspaper. For those of you who are housebound for one reason or another, my advice is to potter round all day. Don't ask people to fetch and carry for you, do it yourself, bend down, stretch up, get up and look out of the window, plant seeds in your window box or herbs in the kitchen – anything that keeps you on the move.

Summary

Do any exercise you enjoy and do it on a regular basis. The regularity is vital. Remember that exercise produces natural opiates which means that you may start the day in a bad mood and end up feeling elated. Everyone can improve their fitness levels and the more unfit you are in the first place, the easier it is to see and feel some progress. Compensate for that sedentary job by burning off stress with exercise.

Chapter 5

BE YOUR OWN PSYCHIATRIST

Food and your relation to it

Don't allow yourself to feel guilty every time you eat something, which is a habit you've acquired from media and magazine hype – not to mention the slimming industry itself who have a vested interest in seducing us to try yet another miracle cure. It may be in the guise of self-help groups, meal replacement drinks or calorie-controlled made-up dishes (which have recently been found to be very high in fat content). They make fortunes from it – we just stay fat! Don't be afraid of food and treat it as illegal – it's delicious, it's necessary for life and should make you feel and look great!

To start with, get over that feeling of self-loathing if you're fat. You're now going to shift it and that's commendable. Don't give in to the tremendous pressure that is put on women to conform to the perfect shape. If you have a consuming need to be accepted and approved of by other people, and to you that means being slim, you have a terrible dilemma within yourself – whether to be that perfect shape and deprive yourself to attain it, or whether to say 'to hell with it, I will eat what I like' and take the consequences. If you follow my eating plan you can start to work on the weight, but meanwhile, try to build up your self-esteem by achieving some other ambitions than that perfect size 12. There are so many interesting classes or hobbies you could start and which are fulfilling in themselves.

Be good to yourself

Take one day at a time – one day without a cigarette is wonderful. Give yourself credit for that ... and on to Day Two. Eat well.

Remember: if you lose your health, it's too late to say 'if only ...' Don't deprive yourself, don't indulge yourself either. Be moderate – it's the happy medium that wins in the end.

Coping with stress

- Concentrate on one thing at a time – you are giving up smoking and you are not going to put on too much weight.

- Talk to someone about your problems – don't let your smoking and weight be the problem.

- Exercise regularly – a walk in the fresh air daily will clear your head.

- Learn to accept that you can't win them all but you can improve the quality of life ...

- A very important factor of which is being happy, and you will feel happier when you've given up smoking and kept your weight down – long term.

- Get off the diet treadmill.

A WORD OF WARNING: REPLACING ONE BAD HABIT WITH ANOTHER

Be careful, if you were using cigarettes as a crutch, that you do not do the same thing with food. Try to do something that will make you feel fulfilled – join a group, take up a new hobby, change your job, but **do it now** – don't wait 'until I'm size 12'. Did comfort-eating ever solve a problem? No!

Sort out your priorities

Everybody is prone to anxiety and tension, whether they are a city mogul rushing from meeting to meeting, airport to airport, or a chocolate-box packer doing a boring repetitive job, so make sure you sort out the priorities important to you. That will help clear your mind.

My suggestion would be, first and foremost, to take up a new hobby that will totally absorb you, leaving you so engrossed that you'll forget to dwell on cigarettes or food. There's a whole range of activities you can take up, from embroidery to painting to carpentry. Why not explore the range and take day or evening classes?

Remember to take your full holiday entitlement, not a day here and a day there, but a full two or three weeks so that you can recharge your batteries.

Work at your own pace

- Decide *when* you want to eat.

- Decide *what* you want to eat.

- Don't let others determine when you need to eat. Just

because the clock says it's lunchtime, it doesn't mean you have to eat then unless you're hungry.

- Don't make this eating healthily and exercising into a big deal. You don't need to invest more money or more time. You need, as with most things, to think ahead and to be prepared, so that life is made easier for you.

Breaking bad habits

Do you bolt your food and not even realize you've eaten? No wonder you soon want to eat again. Like smoking, eating quickly is a bad habit. This is where eating high-fibre food helps.

High-fibre food is roughage or bulk and because it is bulky it takes longer to chew. You need to chew cereals, fruit and vegetables more to allow the food to be swallowed.

Why is this time factor so important? Because when you put something in your mouth, it takes about five minutes before your body registers it – before you start to feel you are eating something and your body starts to become satisfied. If you eat fast, you will have finished your plateful before your body has even begun to register it, and you will be left dissatisfied. A good delaying tactic is to pick up smaller amounts of food on your fork each time.

- Don't read while you're eating – you won't realize you've eaten.

- Don't watch TV while you're eating – you can't concentrate properly on two things at once. So **concentrate on your food**.

- Eat slowly.

I live on my own and I need to watch TV or read whilst I eat. What shall I do?

You'll actually feel much more satisfied if you just concentrate on your food. Make sure you lay the table properly or make yourself up a tray with flowers and a linen tray cloth, use pretty crockery and a serviette and ensure that your view is as nice as you can make it – whether you live in a bedsit or mansion, it's nicer to look at a pretty picture than a bare wall. It's nice, too, to have some pot pourri and a bunch of flowers near you, or to light a scented candle. It's particularly important to indulge yourself if you're always looking after other people – so spoil yourself and make your eating surroundings as luxurious as you can.

Habit strategy

Smoking is a habit you're getting rid of. Now get into the habit of eating properly. Remember that your energy levels are being depleted as you withdraw from the nicotine which stimulates your nervous system, so you really do need to eat a well-balanced diet to replace this energy.

Remember, if you don't concentrate on your food you won't feel you've eaten and you'll always be looking for something else to eat. Whatever you do, don't eat 'on the go' – you'll never remember you've eaten. Sit down, relax and enjoy your meal.

What happens if you fail?

I don't think you will fail because by reading this book you obviously want to change your habit of smoking and/or eating too much. If you're serious about why you want to change and are prepared to watch what you're doing, **you won't fail**.

However, if, in your eyes, failing is, say, eating too much, or eating the wrong sort of food or, dare I say it, having a cigarette, then what you have to keep telling yourself is 'OK,

I'm not perfect, so what? I've been careful about what I've eaten for two weeks and that must count for something.' Give yourself credit for what you have achieved and don't dwell on this temporary lapse.

Don't aim for perfection – why do that to yourself? Tell yourself your next attempt will be better. Even if it's not, see it as a temporary setback not that you, as a person, are a failure – it just isn't true.

Don't waste your feelings on something as negative as guilt. Don't feel remorse – what a waste of emotional energy! Just get right back there and begin again.

You'd take your driving test again – wouldn't you?

You'd get back on your horse which had just thrown you – wouldn't you?

OK, maybe not today, but tomorrow for sure.

Chapter 6

SHOPPING AND COOKING FOR YOUR NEW WAY OF EATING

Menu planning – be prepared

To make life easy for yourself, plan your meals for the week ahead and don't forget to include the fillings you will need for your sandwiches and packed lunches.

You will need to shop twice a week to ensure that you buy fresh fruit and vegetables, so there is no reason why you shouldn't be able to get all the ingredients you'll need for the preparation of all your family's needs.

Don't forget:

1. to go shopping armed with a list, to prevent impulse buys!

2. to make sure you have enough room in your fridge and freezer to accommodate your week's shopping

3. to make maximum storage space in your larder – perhaps you could reorganize your storage section before

embarking on your eating plan to ensure that you get rid of:

- any foods which you won't be needing any more – perhaps you could take them to a jumble sale or charity of some kind
- any tins past their sell-by date
- any unsealed packets that insects might have crawled into
- anything that should have been kept in an air-tight container and has deteriorated.

Once back from the supermarket, cook and freeze portions ahead of time. It's more economical to cook a quantity of food and freeze it for later use. Also, that way, you'll always have something that you can eat as and when you need. **Don't allow yourself to ruin a whole day's carefully planned eating by not having any low-fat snacks readily available.**

Here is a comprehensive shopping list which will allow you to rustle up some nutritious sandwiches, meals and snacks and to make various cereal dishes and pasta meals, incorporating all the nutrients and fibre you need. You won't be starving and need to buy chocolate, crisps, salted nuts, cakes or biscuits.

Shopping chart

Cheese
    Hard cheeses such as Edam or Gouda (you can cut and freeze in portions)
    Low-fat spread or polyunsaturated margarine or olive-oil spread
    Fromage frais and low-fat soft cheese
    Low-fat cottage cheese

Eggs (but don't eat more than three a week)
Milk low-fat, preferably with added calcium
Yogurt: low-fat natural

Tinned food (try to find ones with no added salt or sugar –
read labels carefully)
    Plum tomatoes – unsalted variety
    Fish: sardines, tuna, salmon, mackerel, pilchards
    Beans: baked, broad, butter, flageolot, cannelini, kidney,
    lentils
    Sweetcorn – with no salt or added sugar

Stock cubes – chicken or vegetarian
Fresh or frozen chicken breasts and fish (both of which can
be stored in the freezer)
Herbs – can be frozen
Onions (and spring onions)
Lemons
Fresh fruits in season (see pages 70–71)
Vegetables for nibbling or crudités (see page 53)
Frozen peas, beans, sweetcorn
Mustard
Vinegar
Spices
Peppercorns
Fruit juices – especially freshly squeezed, unsweetened (can
be frozen)
Olive oil (preferably extra virgin) or polyunsaturated veget-
able oil
Bottled water (without bubbles is best for you)
Diet or low-calorie drinks and mixers
White wine (but see alcohol guide)
Yeast extract

Carbohydrate foods
    Stoneground wholemeal bread
    Wholemeal pasta – different shapes, colours and sizes
    Wholegrain rice
    Wholegrain cereals
    Porridge oats

My five golden fruits

Apricots	contain	beta-carotene, selenium, vitamins B and C, calcium
Oranges } Tomatoes }	contain	beta-carotene, vitamins B, C and E, calcium
Blackcurrants	contain	beta-carotene, vitamins B, C and E, calcium
Bananas	contain	beta-carotene, potassium, vitamins B, C and E, calcium
Melons (especially cantaloupe)	contain	beta-carotene, vitamins B, C and E, calcium, iron and potassium

My five golden vegetables

Carrots	contain	beta-carotene, vitamin C and calcium
Spinach	contains	beta-carotene, vitamins C, B, E, K and calcium
Broccoli	contains	beta-carotene, vitamins C, B, E and calcium
Green peppers	contain	beta-carotene, vitamins C, B, E and calcium
{ Watercress	contains	beta-carotene, vitamins C, B, E and calcium
Parsley	contains	vitamins C, B, E, iron and calcium

Seasonal fruits and vegetables

You can see from the list below that there is a variety of both fruits and vegetables available throughout the year.

Fruit

Apples – throughout the year
Apricots – Jan., Feb., May, June, July, Aug., Dec.
Avocado pears – throughout the year
Bananas – throughout the year
Blackberries – June, July, Aug., Sept., Oct.
Blackcurrants – June, July, Aug. – buy as often as you can
Cherries – June, July
Grapes – throughout the year
Gooseberries – July, Aug.
Grapefruit – throughout the year
Greengages – July, Aug.
Lemons – throughout the year
Loganberries – July, Aug. – buy often
Mangoes – Jan. to Sept., inclusive
Melons – throughout the year
Oranges – buy all the time
Peaches – Jan., Feb., Mar., May, June, July, Aug.
Pears – throughout the year
Raspberries – May to Sept., inclusive
Rhubarb – Jan., Feb., Mar., April, May, June, Dec.
Strawberries – April to Oct., inclusive
Tangerines, clementines, satsumas – Jan., Feb., Mar., Oct., Nov., Dec.

When I have suggested fruits such as apricots, blackberries, blackcurrants, loganberries, mangoes, peaches, raspberries, rhubarb, strawberries, satsumas, tangerines which are not available every month of the year, you can substitute some of the following which *are* available throughout the year: apples, bananas, grapes, grapefruit, melons, oranges and pears.

There is a variety of fruit juices to choose from and although – to make life easy for you – I have suggested grapefruit or orange to have with your breakfast, for those who are very well organized, and who are prepared to try new tastes, why not try one of the following: blackcurrant, grape, lemon, lime, pineapple, carrot, mandarin, melon, tangerine, as these are all very high in vitamin C.

Vegetables

Artichokes (globe) – throughout the year
Asparagus – best in early summer
Aubergines – throughout the year
Beans
   broad – April to Aug., inclusive
   french – Jan., Feb., Mar., April, May, June, July, Aug., Nov., Dec.
   runner – May to Oct., inclusive
Broccoli – throughout the year
Brussels sprouts – Jan., Feb., Mar., April, Oct., Nov., Dec.
Cabbage greens – throughout the year
Carrots – throughout the year
Cauliflower – throughout the year
Celery – Jan., Feb., June, July, Aug., Sept., Oct., Nov., Dec.
Chicory – Jan., Feb., Mar., April, May, June, Sept., Oct., Nov., Dec.
Courgettes – throughout the year
Cucumbers – throughout the year
Endive – throughout the year
Fennel – throughout the year
Leeks – Jan., Feb., Mar., April, Aug., Sept., Oct., Nov., Dec.
Lettuce – throughout the year
Mange-tout – April, May, June
Marrows – June, July, Aug., Sept., Oct.
Mushrooms – throughout the year
Onions – throughout the year
Parsnips – Jan., Feb., Mar., April, Sept., Oct., Nov., Dec.
Peas – June to Oct., inclusive – frozen, all year
Peppers – throughout the year
Potatoes
   new – throughout the year, best in summer months
   old – Jan., Feb., Mar., April, May, Sept., Oct., Nov., Dec.

Spinach – throughout the year
Sweetcorn – July, Aug., Sept., Oct.
Swedes – Jan. to May, inclusive, Sept. to Dec. inclusive
Tomatoes – throughout the year
Turnips – throughout the year
Watercress – throughout the year

All the necessary Golden Group vegetables are available throughout the year, i.e. broccoli, cabbage greens, carrots, cauliflower, mushrooms, onions, peppers, potatoes, spinach and watercress – these should be substituted when I have suggested vegetables not in season, i.e. mange-tout.

It is best for a healthy balanced diet to choose a different variety of vegetables daily so that you can take advantage of all the minerals and vitamins they provide.

Never overcook your vegetables as this destroys all the beneficial vitamins and nutrients – microwave or steam is the best way to keep them intact and the vegetables should be eaten immediately. Don't leave them soaking in cold water to get rid of any dirt, just wash in cold water and scrape with a vegetable brush if necessary. Cook potatoes in their skins and try not to peel your root vegetables (the brush should suffice). Best of all is to eat vegetables raw.

If you do boil vegetables, use as little water as possible, and don't pour it away after cooking. Keep it for stock.

Pulses

Pulses, which include split peas, lentils and dried beans are an excellent source of vitamins, calcium, fibre, iron and potassium. They provide vegetable protein which, when combined with wholegrain foods, makes complete protein. Eat them with brown rice, wholemeal toast or wholemeal pasta.

Salads

When making salads or dishes which you place on a bed of lettuce, do make an effort to have a variety of textures and colour. There's such a variety of lettuce to choose from that it really can be a side dish in itself. There's curly red-leaved Lollo Rosso – nice and crispy; Webbs – also crispy; Cos which you can buy in the original long form or the short version called Little Gem, which is short and full of heart leaves packed tightly. Batavia has bitter-tasting curly-type leaves, and cabbage lettuce speaks for itself. There's Iceberg which is also a cabbage lettuce, very crisp and the leaves are tightly packed – like a cabbage – then there's another colourful lettuce with frilly leaves called Red Salad Bowl.

Why not try a different variety whenever you make salad, or a combination of a few different shapes, colours and textures? Add watercress and remember to dress your salad just before eating.

Although the outer leaves are usually discarded they contain most of the beta-carotene, so try to keep them, unless they are very discoloured or tough.

Fish

Fish is a very important food. It is nourishing and easy to clean, prepare and cook. It is an excellent source of protein, vitamins and minerals. Fish oil is polyunsaturated which helps to lower the body's cholesterol level. There are so many different varieties of fish to choose from that you need never get bored.

If you can't get to a fishmonger or to a supermarket that sells fresh fish, use frozen instead. Remember to choose fish which have clear bright eyes (when buying whole fish), a fresh sea smell and shiny skin. When you buy fresh, do cook it as soon as possible or freeze it straight away. Defrost it the night before required, in the fridge.

My five golden fish

Mackerel	contains	vitamin B, calcium, selenium, omega 3 fatty acids
Herring	contains	vitamins B and D, calcium, selenium, omega 3 fatty acids
Sardines	contain	vitamins B and D, calcium, iron and (in tinned fish) zinc, omega 3 fatty acids, selenium
Tuna (tinned)	contains	vitamins B and B6, selenium, calcium and zinc, omega 3 fatty acids
Salmon	contains	vitamins B and D, calcium, selenium and (tinned) zinc, omega 3 fatty acids

In praise of salmon

The flavour is superb, you can bone it easily (unlike herrings). It is delicious and retains all its flavour when it is poached or steamed.

It is a very rich source of omega 3 fatty acids and contains protein, calcium, iron, vitamins A and D, thiamin and riboflavin. Because of the acids it prevents against heart attacks.

It is equally delicious hot or cold.

Complex carbohydrate foods

My five golden complex carbohydrates

Stoneground 100% wholewheat bread	contains	vitamins E and B, zinc, magnesium, niacin, selenium, iron, thiamin and fibre
Porridge oats	contain	bran, iron, niacin, riboflavin, thiamin (vitamin B1) and fibre
Baked potatoes	contain	vitamins C and K, potassium, selenium, fibre
Baked beans	contain	vitamins B, C and K, calcium, beta-carotene, selenium, fibre
Stoneground 100% wholewheat pasta	contains	vitamins B and E, iron, magnesium, thiamin, fibre, niacin

Bread

Only buy stoneground wholewheat or wholemeal bread. Stoneground describes the traditional way of milling the flour, between millstones. This flour contains the most goodness. Wholemeal (wholewheat) bread is made with wholewheat flour, which contains all the wheatgrain, vitamins B and E as well as iron, calcium and fibre.

Wheatgerm

An excellent source of minerals and vitamins. Sprinkle on to your cereal or fruit. It is made from the germ of the wheat.

Pasta

I have suggested eating pasta dishes often in my eating guide as this is a wonderful high-fibre complex carbohydrate and therefore a food that slowly releases energy. No wonder athletes eat this before a race – it provides energy over a lengthy period of time so you won't feel hungry and therefore won't need as much willpower to resist snacking. Pasta contains protein, vitamins B and E, thiamin, niacin, iron, magnesium and fibre.

Don't forget to buy and cook only wholewheat pasta and cook it *al dente* (so it is still slightly firm when you bite it). After you have cooked it, rinse it quickly under the cold tap which gets rid of extra starch. As a rough guide, cook 50 g/ 2 oz (raw weight) per person for a starter or 125 g/4 oz (raw weight) per person for a main course and remember pasta, in itself, is *not* fattening – it's what you put on top that determines the fat content.

Just add plenty of black pepper and a knob of olive oil spread and mix together well – it tastes nice hot or cold. Serve it hot with some vegetables chopped in, or flake in some fish – tuna is good – or serve cold with a crunchy raw salad.

Pasta is cheap to buy and tastes delicious – buy different shapes and try some of the sauces in the recipe section on pages 107–149.

If you must have cheese on top, just sprinkle a small amount of grated Edam over your helping.

Breakfasts

A good, filling, and nutritious breakfast is the answer to resisting a snack at coffee-time or a bag of crisps because you're starving and can't wait till lunch.

You will see, in my suggested menus, the best way to counteract those hunger pangs. On weekdays, I suggest you eat a bowl of vitamin-, calcium- and iron-enriched cereal or a large bowlful of porridge oats with calcium-enriched low-fat milk, or a low-fat natural yogurt. Eat it with a piece of fruit, or drink freshly squeezed juice. At the weekend when the pace is more leisurely I suggest you have a couple of slices of stoneground wholemeal toast, lightly spread with low-fat spread and a spoonful of yeast extract, honey or peanut butter (with no added sugar or salt). Alternatively, try grilled tomatoes on thick slices of wholemeal toast, or poached or boiled eggs (again with wholemeal toast). Don't eat more than 3 eggs per week.

Nuts

These are an excellent source of protein and are rich in minerals and contain vitamins B, C, D and E. They should be used as your main meal protein, not in addition. Try a salad with nuts and seeds. Don't snack on nuts between meals because they won't help you maintain your weight.

Cooking hints

Steaming is the best way of cooking your vegetables, fish or chicken, as none of the nutrients is lost. Besides retaining the flavour of the food, it does away with the need for any oil to be used. Try it, because now that you've given up smoking and your taste buds and sense of smell are returning, you'll see how steaming brings out all the natural flavours and your food won't be water-logged or break up into pieces, which often happens with delicate foods like fish. Steaming is a boon when you're entertaining, too, because vegetables do not need to be drained in a colander.

I find the flower steamer, which unfolds and stands on legs inside the saucepan, to be adequate, but if you need a larger capacity, you'll fare better with a steaming basket which fits on different sizes of pan and can be added to, like the Chinese bamboo steamers. If you have a multi-storey steamer, two or more vegetables can be cooked on a single burner. Put plenty of water in the lower pan, bring to the boil, arrange the vegetables in the steamer and season. Put the steamer in place – well above boiling water level – and cover. Timing depends on the size and thickness of the vegetable. The advantage of the steaming basket is that you can when, say, cooking for a dinner party, cook all the vegetables and/or main course in it, then leave them in the steamer with no detrimental effect, once you have turned off your cooker, until you are ready to serve.

You can place a smaller amount of food between two plates, placed over a saucepan of hot water, if you do not have a steamer.

Microwaving is also a good way to cook healthily, and with minimal loss of nutrients. Remember:

- follow the manufacturer's instructions carefully
- use only clingfilm that is specifically meant for use in a microwave

- leave the food to stand for the recommended time after cooking.

Grilling, poaching, baking and boiling are all suitable cooking methods too. Casserole poultry rather than roast it. This way you can remove the skin before cooking, taking most of the saturated fat with it. Bake fish or chicken in the oven, wrapped loosely in foil with flavourings such as lemon and fresh herbs.

If you must fry, use a non-stick pan – you may not need to add any oil at all. Or stir-fry in a wok. Its steep sides and round bottom mean you need very little oil.

Flavourings

Cut down the amount of salt in your cooking. Salt destroys vitamins. If you must, add salt at the table. Try substituting lemon juice, herbs, spices, pepper and mustard. Salt substitutes contain less real salt than ordinary table salt but most still contain some salt. They are not necessary at all for the average person's diet. Sea salt has other minerals in it too, but is no better than table salt in its general salt content.

If you add artificial sweetener to, say, rhubarb, add it after cooking. Otherwise you will get a horrible bitter taste.

Dressings and dips

Make dressings from extra virgin olive oil and lemon juice, or fromage frais or low-fat yogurt mixed with lemon juice. Use very low-fat soft cheese for dips.

Extra virgin olive oil is a greenish colour. It is derived from the first, cold pressing of the olives. It is worth every penny. It is often mixed with olive oil made from subsequent pressings, which makes it less pungent, less thick and less expensive.

Other oils which can be used for salads include safflower, sesame, grapeseed, sunflower and soya. Then there are the speciality oils such as walnut oil. All these oils are polyunsaturated and help control the cholesterol level in your blood.

Herbs

Why not make a stab at growing your own herbs – all you need is some sun. As you probably know, the more you pick your herbs, the more they grow, so you get plenty of return for your efforts and it's great just being able to reach out and pick a sprig of mint or a handful of chives to add to your meals. Placed on your sunniest window ledge, a few pots of herbs won't take up much room and are pretty to look at as they grow. Start off by growing parsley, basil, mint, chives and rosemary, which adds a lovely flavour to your chicken and fish dishes. Parsley is the only one which needs shade, so remember not to place it with your other herbs who love the sun. Parsley is a very rich source of vitamin C. I have added it to most of my recipes.

Chapter 7

THE 30-DAY
EATING GUIDE

═══════════════════

As I have said earlier in the book, when you first give up smoking, the nicotine withdrawal causes you to crave more carbohydrates to keep up your accustomed levels of the chemical serotonin, which creates feelings of elation and happiness. Most people giving up cigarettes consume about 300 extra calories a day for at least four weeks. In this chapter I have suggested an eating plan which should deal with those cravings while limiting the extra calories. Remember that the plan goes hand-in-hand with increased exercise.

It is based on

● foods which are thought to be cancer-preventative

● foods which are packed with vitamin C which is extremely helpful when you are withdrawing from tobacco. It protects you against heart disease and also gives you the extra energy you need to combat withdrawal symptoms

● foods rich in omega 3 fatty acids which help to maintain the condition of your arteries and lower your blood fats thus reducing the risk of blood clots which cause fatal heart attacks – this is vital for smokers. Omega 3 fatty acids are also thought to be cancer-preventative

- foods which are high in fibre, because these are the ones which fill you up and leave you feeling full-up longer – they are slow-release foods which keep your energy levels high so the need to snack in between meals is reduced. Fibre is also thought to reduce the cholesterol level in your blood

- foods from my Five Golden Groups (see pages 21–22) – foods rich in vitamin C, beta-carotene, selenium, vitamin E and complex carbohydrates.

During this 30-day period, you will make 1½ sandwiches each day if you are a woman, 2 if you are a man. You will eat 1 at lunchtime and the remainder whenever your particular danger time is. You will take carrots with you to work (or have them readily available at home) to nibble on when the hunger-pangs begin or when you need a cigarette. You'll drink very low-fat milk enriched with calcium. You'll use low-fat spread which is high in polyunsaturates on your bread. You'll try not to drink alcohol daily – for health reasons – but if you do, you'll follow the recommended alcohol levels.

After the initial 30-day period, if you feel you can cope during danger times or your will-power is strong, you can revert to one sandwich a day but really unless you're gaining weight, why not carry on as you are? The extra half-sandwich will not do you any harm, so long as you keep your fillings fat- and sugar-free, and the calories will certainly get burned up during the day. Do keep up your extra exercise routine – this should be easy to do as you will become fitter and enjoy the extra activity each day.

Whatever you do, don't get depressed – if you've not been as good as you would have liked with either your giving up smoking or your eating. Just try again. It's like going through a revolving door – if you don't come out of the right space first time, you'll do it on the second attempt. The main thing is **be determined. If you are determined you'll do it.**

Do it now!

Good Luck!

Monday

Breakfast: Freshly squeezed grapefruit juice
(+ 1 whole orange for men)
Porridge oats with water or calcium-enriched milk, sprinkled with one or two tablespoons of natural wheatgerm

Danger time: Carrots

Lunch: Sandwiches filled with sardines (tinned in brine or water), mashed with olive oil and lemon juice, sliced tomato and chopped parsley
1 orange (2 oranges for men)
If you didn't have milk on your porridge oats, a natural low-fat yogurt

Danger time: Sandwich and apple

Before dinner: Glass of tomato juice (see recipe on page 149)

Dinner: Green and red pepper salad with spring onion and chopped parsley
Grilled mackerel
Spinach and cauliflower
Melon and strawberries

Note on quantities:

Sandwich = 1½ rounds for women, 2 rounds for men.

Pitta bread = 1½ large size or 3 picnic size for women, 2 large or 4 picnic size for men.

Remember to save part of the sandwich to eat at the afternoon danger time.

Tuesday

Breakfast: Orange juice (men: add 1 whole orange)
Bowl of bite-size shredded wheat, milk with fresh blackcurrants

Danger time: Carrots

Lunch: Brown pitta breads filled with kidney and flageolet beans, spring onions, dressing and chopped parsley
Kiwi fruit and an apple

Danger time: Sandwich and pear

Before dinner: Glass of tomato juice

Dinner: Baked trout
Grilled (or microwaved) mushrooms, cauliflower, spring greens
Orange (men: 2), fromage frais and blackberries, add 1 tablespoon natural wheatgerm

Wednesday

Breakfast: Fresh orange and grapefruit segments (men: whole orange and $\frac{1}{2}$ grapefruit)
2 slices of stoneground wholemeal toast, olive oil or polyunsaturated low-fat spread, sliced fresh tomatoes

Danger time: Carrots

Lunch: Pitta filled with 2 bananas, sliced, and curd cheese, sprinkled with natural wheatgerm
Orange (men: 2) and grapes

Danger time: Sandwich and apple

Before dinner: Glass of tomato juice

Dinner: Melon
Sea Bass with tarragon (see recipe, page 118)
Microwaved or steamed mushrooms, broccoli
Rhubarb and banana bake (see recipe, page 147)
Pear, low-fat natural yogurt and blackberries

Thursday

Breakfast: Home-made fruit muesli
Fresh orange

Danger time: Carrots

Lunch: Sardine sandwich with sliced tomatoes, chopped parsley
Cherries and kiwi fruit

Danger time: Sandwich + 1 banana

Before dinner: Glass of tomato juice

Dinner: $\frac{1}{2}$ grapefruit
Chicken fillet baked in the oven with herbs
Fresh spinach and courgettes
Bananas in orange juice (see recipe, page 147) with 1 tablespoon natural wheatgerm
Apple and orange (men: 2 oranges)

Friday

Breakfast: Orange juice (men: add 1 whole orange)
Bowl of bran cereal with milk

Danger time: Carrots

Lunch: Tuna sandwich with lettuce, cucumber, tomato, spring onion, chopped parsley, dressing

Danger time: sandwich, pear and a banana

Before dinner: Glass of wine or tomato juice

Dinner: Wholewheat pasta spirals with tuna (see recipe, page 131) and mushrooms
Spinach salad with garlic and carrots
Slice of fresh pineapple and strawberries with low-fat fromage frais, and 1 tablespoon wheatgerm

Saturday

Breakfast: Orange juice (men: add 1 whole orange)
Grilled tomatoes on 2 slices toast, seasoned with ground black pepper

Danger time:	1 slice toast and banana
Lunch:	Wholewheat spaghetti and tomato sauce (see recipe, page 134) Green salad Orange
Danger time:	Strawberries and low-fat yogurt
Before dinner:	Glass of wine
Dinner:	Grapefruit and orange segments Mediterranean fish casserole (see recipe, page 120) Spinach and carrots Fresh fruit salad Fromage frais and wheatgerm

Sunday

Breakfast:	Orange juice (men: add 1 whole orange) 2 poached eggs on two pieces of toast
Danger time:	Banana
Lunch:	Jacket potatoes with fromage frais and chives Pepper salad (see recipe, page 139) Orange (men: 2)
Danger time:	Bowl of strawberries with fromage frais
Before dinner:	Glass of wine
Dinner	Gazpacho Chicken kebabs (see recipe, page 124) Wholegrain rice and salad Peaches in orange juice

Week 2 – should start to get easier.

Monday

Breakfast:	Grapefruit juice (men: add 1 whole orange) Bowl of raisin wheats, low-fat yogurt and wheatgerm
Danger time:	Carrots
Lunch:	Pitta bread filled with low-fat natural cottage cheese, add sweetcorn, peas, chopped haricot beans, spring onion, chopped parsley, fromage frais dressing Blackcurrants and redcurrants
Danger time:	Pitta and 1 whole orange (men: 2)
Before dinner:	Glass of tomato juice
Dinner:	Carrot soup Baked potato with lentils Broccoli and cauliflower Melon and strawberries Tangerines and pear

Tuesday

Breakfast:	Orange juice (men: add 1 whole orange) Fruit and nut muesli, wheatgerm Add fresh apricots if available
Danger time:	Carrots
Lunch:	Tinned salmon sandwich with lettuce, cucumber, tomato, chopped parsley, spring onion
Danger time:	Sandwich + orange (men: 2)

Before dinner: Glass of tomato juice

Dinner: ½ grapefruit
Bean bake (see recipe, page 127)
Banana crunch (see recipe, page 146)
Kiwis and cherries

Wednesday

Breakfast: Grapefruit juice (men: add 1 whole orange)
Porridge oats, wheatgerm

Danger time: Carrots

Lunch: Pitta bread spread with yeast extract, with watercress, cherry tomatoes, spring onion
Apple, tangerines

Danger time: Pitta, banana

Before dinner: Glass of tomato juice

Dinner: Mushroom salad
Spiced chicken in yogurt (see recipe, page 123)
Cauliflower and broccoli
Grapefruit and orange segments
Grapes

Thursday

Breakfast: Bowl of berries, low-fat yogurt, wheatgerm
Slice of toast, olive oil spread and yeast extract

Danger time: Carrots

Lunch: Tinned mackerel sandwich, sweetcorn, peas, spring onion, chopped parsley
Orange (men: 2)

Danger time: Sandwich, peach

Before dinner: Glass of tomato juice

Dinner: Melon
Baked fish (see recipe, page 118)
Blackcurrant water ice
Banana and grapes

Friday

Breakfast: Fruit muesli with strawberries (men: add 1 whole orange), add wheatgerm

Danger time: Carrots

Lunch: Pitta bread filled with broad beans and butter beans, spring onions, chopped parsley, dressed
Satsumas

Danger time: Pitta, orange

Before dinner: Glass of tomato juice

Dinner: Carottes râpées (see recipe, page 129)
Haddock florentine (see recipe, page 120)
Haricot beans and steamed mushrooms
Raspberries and low-fat fromage frais
Orange and apple

Saturday

Breakfast: Orange juice (men: add 1 whole orange)
Scrambled eggs (2) on toast

Danger time: Carrots

Lunch: Baked beans on toast
Fresh tomatoes
Low-fat natural yogurt with wheatgerm
Orange (men: 2)

Danger time: Piece of fruit

Before dinner: Glass of wine

Dinner: Tomato salad with olive oil, chopped parsley and sliced onion
Baked gingered chicken (see recipe, page 121)
Broccoli, endive salad
Peaches with raspberry sauce (see recipe, page 148)

Sunday

Breakfast: Grapefruit and orange juice mixed
Grilled tomatoes

Danger time: Carrots

Lunch: Cauliflower cheese
Mushrooms and haricot beans

Danger time: Slice of toast with yeast extract
Piece of fruit

Before dinner: Glass of wine

Dinner: Grilled spiced jumbo prawns
Wholegrain rice and large green
salad
Melon, strawberries and low-fat
yogurt with wheatgerm

Week 3

Monday

Breakfast: Grapefruit juice (men: add 1 whole
orange)
2 Weetabix with banana, milk and
wheatgerm

Danger time: Carrots

Lunch: Pitta bread filled with tuna and
kidney beans, endive, spring onions
and chopped parsley, dressed
Orange (men: 2)

Danger time: Pitta, pear

Before dinner: Glass of tomato juice

Dinner: Cucumber and tomato salad,
chopped parsley
Baked trout with fennel
Broccoli and carrots
Melon and rhubarb with low-fat
fromage frais, sprinkled with
blackcurrants

Tuesday

Breakfast: Muesli with nuts and seeds. Add
wheatgerm (see recipe, page 108)
Orange juice (men: add 1 whole
orange)

Danger time: Carrots

Lunch: Tinned salmon sandwich with chicory, tomato, spring onion and chopped parsley, lemon juice
Low-fat yogurt, pear

Danger time: Sandwich, apple

Before dinner: Glass of tomato juice

Dinner: Green bean salad, with chopped parsley (see recipe, page 139)
Mackerel with pepper sauce (see recipe, page 132)
Spinach, french beans
Bowl of blackcurrants and strawberries

Wednesday

Breakfast: Orange juice (men: add 1 whole orange)
Bowl of puffed wheat with sliced banana and wheatgerm

Danger time: Carrots

Lunch: Tuna sandwich with haricot beans, lemon juice, chopped parsley
Orange (men: 2)

Danger time: Sandwich, grapes

Before dinner: Glass of tomato juice

Dinner: $\frac{1}{2}$ grapefruit with ginger
Greenbrae rice (see recipe, page 130)
Spinach salad
Rhubarb and baked banana, with strawberries and low-fat natural yogurt
Apple

Thursday

Breakfast:	Grapefruit and orange juice, mixed (men: add 1 whole orange) Bowl of bran cereal, milk, wheatgerm, dot with fresh strawberries
Danger time:	Carrots
Lunch:	Tomato soup (see recipe, page 115) Watercress sandwich with sliced mushrooms and spring onions, olive oil Banana
Danger time:	Sandwich, orange (men: 2)
Before dinner:	Glass of tomato juice
Dinner:	½ grapefruit Fresh salmon steak Beans and spinach Redcurrants and mango with fromage frais (see recipe, page 147)

Friday

Breakfast:	Orange juice (men: add 1 whole orange) Shredded wheat with milk, wheatgerm and banana
Danger time:	Carrots
Lunch:	Pitta bread filled with low-fat soft cheese and fresh figs Apple
Danger time:	Pitta, orange (men: 2)
Before dinner:	Glass of tomato juice

Dinner: ½ grapefruit
Sweet chicken (see recipe, page 123)
Broccoli
Strawberries and blackberries,
low-fat yogurt

Saturday

Breakfast: Orange juice (men: add 1 whole
orange)
1 poached egg on toast
1 toast with grilled tomato

Danger time: Carrots

Lunch: Three bean salad: kidney, cannellini
and butter beans, dressed. Add
spring onion, chopped parsley
Green salad

Danger time: Piece of fruit

Before dinner: Glass of wine

Dinner: Tomato salad, dressed
Chicken with mustard sauce
Chicory provençale (see recipe, page
126)
Mango and orange slices decorated
with pieces of kiwi and mixed colour
grapes, eaten with fromage frais and
wheatgerm

Sunday

Breakfast: Grapefruit juice (men: add 1 whole
orange)
Sardines and tomatoes on toast

Danger time: Carrots

Lunch:	Vegetable curry Wholegrain rice Strawberries and yogurt with wheatgerm
Danger time:	Piece of fruit (men: 2 oranges)
Before dinner:	Glass of wine
Dinner:	Melon and fresh figs Fennel and Edam bake (see recipe, page 129) Mélange of vegetables, broccoli and cauliflower florets, peas, mushrooms and mange-tout Fresh pineapple, raspberries and kiwis

Week 4

Monday

Breakfast:	Grapefruit juice Bowl of porridge oats with milk
Danger time:	Carrots
Lunch:	Peanut butter and curd cheese sandwich Orange and banana (men: 2 oranges)
Danger time:	Sandwich, pear
Before dinner:	Glass of tomato juice
Dinner:	Onion salad Mozzarella salad (see recipe, page 142) As many berries as you like with fromage frais and wheatgerm, slice of melon

Tuesday

Breakfast:	Mixed orange and grapefruit juice (men: add 1 orange) Bowl of bite-size shredded wheat, milk and wheatgerm
Danger time:	Carrots
Lunch:	Chicken fillet sandwich with bamboo shoots and watercress, spring onion, chopped parsley, tomato
Danger time:	Sandwich, orange (men: 2)
Before dinner:	Glass of tomato juice
Dinner:	Grapefruit and orange segments, garnished with fresh mint Tabbouleh (see recipe, page 131) Spinach salad Fresh mango, low-fat yogurt

Wednesday

Breakfast:	Grapefruit juice (men: add 1 whole orange) Bowl of Weetabix with milk
Danger time:	Carrots
Lunch:	Tuna and tomato sandwich, with cucumber, tomato, spring onion and chopped parsley, lemon juice
Danger time:	Sandwich, pear, orange (men: 2 oranges)
Before dinner:	Glass of tomato juice

Dinner: Fish casserole
Broccoli, cauliflower
Banana and rhubarb with low-fat
fromage frais and wheatgerm

Thursday

Breakfast: Orange juice (men: add 1 whole
orange)
Bowl of bran cereal, milk

Danger time: Carrots

Lunch: Edam and tomato sandwich with
lettuce, cucumber, spring onion and
chopped parsley

Danger time: Sandwich, satsumas (men: satsumas
+ 1 orange)

Before dinner: Glass of tomato juice

Dinner: Tomato salad
Sea-bass with tarragon (see recipe,
page 118)
Cauliflower and beans
Baked apple (see recipe, page 146)
with low-fat yogurt and wheatgerm

Friday

Breakfast: Orange juice (men: add 1 whole
orange)
Porridge oats, wheatgerm

Danger time: Carrots

Lunch: Tomato sandwich, dressed, add
watercress, spring onion, chopped
parsley

Danger time: Sandwich, cherries

Before dinner:	Glass of tomato juice
Dinner:	Butter bean salad
	Moules marinières
	Salad
	Fresh peaches and grapes
	Low-fat fromage frais

Saturday

Breakfast:	Orange juice (men: add 1 whole orange)
	Scrambled egg on toast (use olive oil spread to cook the egg), tomato
Danger time:	Piece of fruit
Lunch:	Salade niçoise (see recipe, page 141)
	Peach, grapes
Danger time:	Piece of fruit
Before dinner:	Glass of wine
Dinner:	Leeks vinaigrette
	Bouillabaisse
	Green salad
	Fresh pineapple, fromage frais and wheatgerm

Sunday

Breakfast:	Orange juice (men: add 1 whole orange)
	Porridge oats and berries
Danger time:	Piece of fruit
Lunch:	Fish pie
	Cauliflower
Danger time:	Piece of fruit

Before dinner: Glass of wine

Dinner: Corn on the cob
                      Melted olive oil spread
                      Salmon trout, fennel and peas
                      Hot fruit salad

Day 29 Things should be getting much easier now that
you're in a routine. If you don't need it, cut out the danger-
time snacks, but only when you can.

Monday

Breakfast: Juice – grapefruit or orange (men:
                      add 1 whole orange)
                      Bran flakes, banana

Danger time: Carrots

Lunch: Sardine sandwich with tomatoes and
                      watercress

Danger time: Piece of fruit (and half sandwich if
                      you need it)

Before dinner: Glass of tomato juice

Dinner: Tomato salad, dressed, with
                      chopped parsley
                      Pasta with tuna
                      Green salad
                      Fresh fruit, low-fat yogurt with
                      wheatgerm

Day 30

Tuesday

Breakfast: Orange juice (men: add 1 whole
                      orange)
                      Porridge oats and milk, wheatgerm

Danger time:	Carrots
Lunch:	Tuna and tomato sandwich with lettuce, cucumber, spring onion, lemon juice, garnished with parsley
Danger time:	Piece of fruit (half-sandwich if needed)
Before dinner:	Glass of tomato juice
Dinner:	Mushrooms à la Grècque Baked trout Spinach and cauliflower Melon and raspberries, low-fat yogurt

Well done! You've made it this far. By now, the worst cravings should be over and you should find that you can do without some of the danger-time snacks.

What follows are some sample menus to help you keep up the good work now that the first crucial month is over.

Sample menus

Breakfast:	Orange juice or whole orange Puffed wheat with calcium-enriched low-fat milk and sliced banana
Lunch:	Tinned salmon sandwich with sliced cucumber and tomato Pear, grapes
Dinner:	Baked sea bass Courgettes, broccoli and carrots Fruit salad and low-fat natural yogurt

Breakfast:	Tomato juice Porridge oats made with water
Lunch:	Kidney and cannellini beans mixed with olive oil and lemon juice, parsley and sliced spring onions (remember to pack a fork if you are taking this to the office) Grapes, kiwi fruit
Dinner:	Salmon steaks Tomato and onion salad Broccoli Orange, apple

* * *

Breakfast:	Freshly-squeezed orange juice Porridge oats made with water
Lunch:	Banana sandwich on stoneground wholemeal bread cut thick, spread with low-fat margarine Pear, grapes
Dinner:	Tomato salad Chicken in yogurt and spices Wholegrain rice Broccoli, beans Low-fat fromage frais with orange and strawberries

* * *

Breakfast:	Freshly squeezed grapefruit juice Porridge oats, made with water Tea or coffee
Lunch:	Chicken salad sandwich on stoneground wholemeal bread spread lightly with low-fat spread Low-fat yogurt, orange

Dinner: Melon
Wholewheat pasta with home-made
tomato sauce (see recipe, page 134)
Broccoli and cauliflower florets with
some of the home-made tomato
sauce poured over
Fresh fruit

*   *   *

Breakfast: Freshly-squeezed pink grapefruit
juice
Home-made muesli (see recipe, page
108)
Sliced orange

Lunch: Sardine and tomato sandwich on
stoneground wholemeal bread
spread with low-fat spread
Orange, kiwi fruit

Dinner: Home-made tomato soup (see
recipe, page 115)
Baked trout with vegetables
Fromage frais with fresh
strawberries or a banana

*   *   *

Breakfast: Fruit juice
Raisin wheats with calcium-enriched
low-fat milk

Lunch: Egg and tomato sandwich on
stoneground wholemeal bread with
low-fat spread
Pear, a few raisins

Dinner: Grilled mackerel
Spinach, beans
Fresh pineapple slice with low-fat
natural yogurt, grapes

Breakfast: Tomato juice
2 Weetabix with calcium-enriched milk and sliced banana (this is also very nice hot – put in microwave on medium for 2 minutes)

Lunch: Tomato sandwich in stoneground wholemeal bread, thickly cut, with low-fat spread (if you're not going to breathe on anyone at work, add sliced spring onions)
Fresh pear, kiwi or apple
Low-fat yogurt

Dinner: Turkey breasts baked in the oven with herbs
Spinach and carrots
Baked apple (see recipe, page 146)
Orange

* * *

Breakfast: Tomato juice
Bran cereal with calcium-enriched low-fat milk

Lunch: Tuna fish sandwich with tomatoes and cucumber on stoneground wholemeal bread with low-fat spread
Apple and orange

Dinner: Grilled grapefruit
Vegetable curry (see recipe, page 128) with large green salad dressed with lemon juice and extra virgin olive oil
Wholegrain rice
Low-fat fromage frais, banana and blackberries

Breakfast: Bowl of bite-size shredded wheat
with calcium-enriched low-fat milk
Orange juice

Lunch: Edam cheese and tomato sandwich
with watercress on stoneground
wholemeal bread, cut thick with low-
fat spread
Small bunch of green or black
grapes, pear

Dinner: Moules marinières
Wholegrain rice and salad
Rhubarb and banana cooked in
microwave on medium for 2
minutes, orange

OVEN TEMPERATURE CHART

Gas Mark	°F	°C
½	250	130
1	275	140
2	300	150
3	325	170
4	350	180
5	375	190
6	400	200
7	425	220
8	450	230
9	475	240

Chapter 8

RECIPES

I have used lots of garlic, oily fish, pasta, grains, legumes, deep-coloured vegetables and olive oil as these have recently been shown to have beneficial effects in areas such as lowering blood cholesterol and combatting cancer (the so-called Mediterranean diet).

Remember that fresh simple ingredients in season, with their beautiful colours, can look and taste sensational. Think of the effect of aubergines, olives, tomatoes and parsley, carrots, grapes, berries and melon. It's so important to eat food that not only tastes good but looks good too. It lifts your spirits. Why shouldn't you treat yourself to food that looks good?

Breakfast

OATMEAL PORRIDGE

(serves 4)

> $1\frac{1}{2}$ pints/$3\frac{1}{2}$ cups water
> 150 g/5 oz/$\frac{2}{3}$ cup medium oatmeal
> Salt

Bring the water to boil in a heavy pan. Make sure it is bubbling well so that the oatmeal does not clot when stirred in. Sprinkle in the oatmeal slowly. Stir with wooden spoon until smooth. Lower the heat, cover the pan and simmer very gently for 10 minutes. Add a good sprinkling of salt, cover again and simmer for another 10 minutes.

This porridge, with a glass of orange juice and a carton of low-fat yogurt makes a perfectly balanced breakfast. It contains calcium and vitamins B and C. It is low in fat and high in soluble fibre. This is the breakfast I choose when I know I'm not going to be able to eat lunch till latish or not have a snack in between. It keeps me going for hours without hunger pangs. (You could keep the yogurt to eat later if you think you might face a danger time during the morning.)

HOME-MADE MUESLI

(serves 4)

Lemon juice
1 apple, cored and chopped
125 g/4 oz/½ cup rolled oats
2 tablespoons each bran and natural wheatgerm
25 g/1 oz/¼ cup dried peaches

25 g/1 oz/¼ cup raisins
25 g/1 oz/⅛ cup demerara sugar
4 tablespoons chopped nuts
Sunflower seeds
15 cl/¼ pint/½ cup low-fat, calcium-enriched milk

Pour lemon juice over the chopped apple to stop it discolouring. Mix your oats, bran, wheatgerm, peaches, raisins and sugar with chopped nuts and sunflower seeds. Mix in the apple and milk.

You can vary your muesli by adding dried pears, prunes or apricots or changing your variety of chopped nuts. Any soft fruit in season makes a nice change, and you can always add a fresh banana and some grapes or some stewed fruit for a change.

Snack lunches

Here are some suggestions for sandwich fillings, some of which could also be eaten as salads on their own. If so, transport them to work in plastic containers – bring your bread or pitta spread with olive oil low-fat spread and eat separately with the fillings. Remember to pack a fork!

I have also given some ideas for people who are working from home and can make hot snacks like baked beans on toast. Of course if you're lucky enough to have a microwave at work and prefer a hot snack lunch, then use these recipe ideas.

Sandwich fillings

TUNA AND KIDNEY BEANS

Mix tuna and kidney beans together and add a teaspoon of olive oil and a sliced spring onion. Eat with some sliced green peppers.

LOW-FAT CHEESE AND DRIED FIGS

Chop the dried figs and mix into the cheese. Eat with banana and kiwi fruit cut in half.

TINNED SALMON AND CHICORY

Mash the salmon, including the bones (a good source of calcium). Chop the endive in cubes and add, with a teaspoon of olive oil. Eat with watercress and tomato salad with spring onion, followed by an apple.

SARDINE AND WATERCRESS

Mash the sardines (canned in brine or water), add a teaspoon of olive oil and top with watercress and spring onion. Eat with sliced green peppers and follow with a couple of tangerines.

COTTAGE CHEESE AND FRESH APRICOTS

Mix low-fat natural cottage cheese with 3 fresh apricots, cut in halves. Follow with fresh pear.

CHICKEN FILLET WITH MUSHROOMS AND WATERCRESS

Slice as many fresh mushrooms as you need for your slices of bread and add watercress and spring onion on top of cold poached chicken. Follow with an orange.

MACKEREL AND HARICOT BEANS

Place haricot beans dressed with one teaspoon olive oil on top of tinned mackerel fillets. Add spring onion slices. Follow with a peach.

FRESH POACHED SALMON OR SALMON TROUT

Squeeze lemon onto fresh poached salmon (save a piece from your evening meal). Eat with crunchy cauliflower and bean salad. Follow with some grapes.

Here are some other sandwich ideas, for lunches or picnics. Instead of using low-fat spread, use low-fat cream cheese.

- Tuna and spring onion
- Banana and chopped dates
- Banana and chopped figs
- Chopped dates or figs

- Peanut butter
- Salad
- Watercress and sliced mushrooms
- Just sprinkle on the cream/curd cheese some sultanas or raisins
- Sliced tomato and cucumber
- Tinned salmon and chopped cucumber
- Hard-boiled eggs and slices of tomato
- Cold flaked fish
- Turkey and watercress
- Grated carrot and a few raisins
- Chopped celery and apple and a few raisins or walnuts
- Bamboo shoots, watercress and sliced mushrooms

Pitta bread fillings

Two bananas, sliced – one in each pocket. Add curd cheese.

Brown rice and kidney beans, dressed with olive oil and add chopped parsley.

Three beans – cannellini, flageolet and kidney, dressed with olive oil and chopped parsley.

Broad beans and butter beans, dressed with olive oil, add spring onion and chopped parsley.

New potatoes with low-fat natural yogurt, spring onions and chopped parsley, add mustard and cress and olive oil.

Chicken and salad dressed with low-fat natural yogurt, olive oil, lemon juice, spring onion and chopped parsley.

Peanut butter and curd cheese – spread each pocket with curd cheese and add peanut butter (the kind without added sugar).

Tuna, drained of oil, with haricot beans and spring onions, dressed with lemon juice and olive oil and garnished with chopped parsley.

Low-fat cottage cheese with sweetcorn and peas, add olive oil, chopped parsley and spring onion.

Low-fat cottage cheese with carrots and celery, dressed with olive oil, spring onion and chopped parsley.

Curd cheese with peaches. Spread the curd cheese around the pocket and fold in the sliced peaches.

Cold new potatoes (left from the night before), cut in halves, with some sweetcorn and peas, dressed with olive oil, garnished with chopped parsley and spring onions.

Mixed lettuce leaves, cherry tomatoes, slices of carrots, spring onion, dressed with olive oil, lemon juice and chopped parsley.

Yeast extract and lots of fresh watercress, a few cherry tomatoes and spring onion.

Brown rice, sweetcorn and peas, dressed with olive oil, garnished with chopped parsley and spring onions.

Lots of fresh green watercress with sliced fresh mushrooms and spring onion.

Bamboo shoots, watercress, sliced fresh mushrooms, chopped spring onion, dressed with soy sauce.

Sliced green pepper with sweetcorn and onions, dressed with olive oil and chopped parsley.

Brown rice and mixed green and red peppers, olive oil, spring onion.

Pitta bread

Buy brown rather than white. Slit along the edge
to make a pocket for a variety of fillings, or cut in
half for two pockets.

Snack lunches at home for one

HERRING ROES ON TOAST

Grill the roes and add mustard. Place on 2 pieces of toasted
stoneground wholemeal bread. Sprinkle with chopped
parsley. Follow with an orange.

CAULIFLOWER CHEESE

Break the cauliflower into florets and mash. Melt 15 g/½ oz
grated Edam cheese over the top and sprinkle with chopped
parsley. Follow with two tangerines.

BAKED BEANS ON TOAST

Have one slice of toast and two later whenever it's your
danger time, or two slices now and one later. Spread with
low-fat spread and pour over the beans. Add a sliced tomato
and chopped parsley. Follow with a pear.

COTTAGE CHEESE WITH SWEETCORN AND PEPPERS

(serves 1)

> 125 g/4 oz/¼ cup cottage cheese
> 50 g/2 oz/¼ cup tinned sweetcorn, drained
> Chopped green and red peppers
> Parsley

Mix together the sweetcorn and the cottage cheese and add chopped peppers. Sprinkle with parsley. Follow with an orange.

SARDINE SPECIAL

This sardine recipe is good to use either for a snack at home or as a pitta filling. It is a good idea to have sardines as a lunchtime snack at least once a week as they are rich in calcium and vitamin D (which you need for strong bones and teeth) and vitamin B12 which helps your nervous system and blood. Another benefit is they contain niacin which supplies us with the necessary energy.

(serves 2/3)

> 1 × 200 g/7 oz can of   1 hard-boiled egg
>   sardines in oil   Lemon juice
> 125 g/4 oz low-fat cream   Black pepper
>   cheese

Mash together the sardines in oil and cream cheese, adding the chopped hard-boiled egg, lemon juice and pepper.

Why not try sardines on top of grilled tomatoes, sprinkled with parsley?

Soups and starters

HOME-MADE MINESTRONE

(serves 4)

2 medium onions, sliced
1 garlic clove, chopped
2 tbsp olive oil
Celery, chopped
Carrots, chopped
Tin of flageolet beans, drained
1.2 l/2 pints/5 cups chicken or vegetable stock

French beans
Courgettes, sliced
Broccoli florets
Peas
Freshly ground black pepper
Chopped parsley for garnish

Fry in olive oil the onion and garlic clove, adding chopped celery and carrots. Sweat with lid on for 5 minutes. Add the tin of flageolet beans and cover with stock. Bring to the boil and add the french beans. Simmer for about 1 hour then add the courgettes, broccoli florets and peas. Cook for further 20 minutes. Season with black pepper and add parsley before serving.

If this soup makes up your entire meal, add some grated Edam cheese and eat with a stoneground wholemeal roll.

TOMATO SOUP

(serves 4)

1 garlic clove, chopped
1 large onion, sliced
Olive oil
Basil leaves
1 large tin tomatoes (in summer use fresh tomatoes and skin)

Freshly ground black pepper
Vegetable stock cube
1 tbsp tomato purée

Cook the chopped garlic and onion in a little olive oil, adding some fresh basil. Add the chopped tomatoes and black pepper. Add a vegetable stock cube and the tomato purée and simmer for an hour or so. Add water as necessary. Garnish with chopped basil.

CARROT SOUP

(serves 4)

1 medium potato, peeled and chopped	¼ tsp coriander seed, crushed
1 medium leek, washed and finely chopped	1 vegetable stock cube
8 carrots, sliced	Parsley, chopped
90 cl/1¾ pints/3½ cups water	

Bring all the ingredients to the boil in a large saucepan then simmer till vegetables are *al dente* (slightly firm when bitten). Blend until smooth then re-heat in the saucepan. Add more chopped parsley and serve with a stoneground wholemeal roll if this is your lunchtime meal.

GAZPACHO

(serves 4)

500 g/1 lb/2 cups tomatoes	4 tbsp wine vinegar
1 yellow pepper, chopped	4 tbsp olive oil
1 onion, chopped	2 tbsp water
2 cloves garlic, crushed	Celery, chopped
Freshly ground black pepper	½ cucumber, chopped

Put into a blender the tomatoes, most of the pepper and onion and the crushed garlic. Blend till smooth and add black pepper, vinegar, oil and water. Put in the fridge for a couple of hours, and serve with the remaining chopped onion, yellow pepper, cucumber and celery.

BUTTER BEAN SOUP

250 g/8 oz/1 cup dried butter beans	2 celery stalks, chopped
2 tbsp olive oil	Small tin of tomatoes
1 large onion, chopped	$\frac{1}{2}$ tsp chopped basil leaves
2 garlic cloves, chopped	Freshly ground black pepper
Small bay leaf	Broccoli florets
4 carrots, chopped	

Bring the butter beans to the boil in plenty of water. Let this sit, with the lid on, for about an hour then bring back to the boil and cook for half an hour.

Fry in olive oil the onion and garlic, add the bay leaf, then the carrots and celery. Cook for 2 minutes and add to the beans, with the tomatoes, chopped basil leaves and black pepper. Add the broccoli florets. Let the soup simmer but don't overcook – the vegetables should be *al dente* (still firm when bitten).

Finally, here are three fruit starters suitable for the smartest dinner party.

MELON COCKTAIL

Take three different coloured melons and cut the flesh into balls. Sprinkle on a little ginger.

HOT FRUIT COCKTAIL

(serves 2)

1 grapefruit
2 oranges

Segment the oranges and the grapefruit. Place in an ovenproof dish and grill for a few minutes.

Serve with cold natural low-fat yogurt, sprinkled with chopped mint.

This can be served as a starter but is equally good as a dessert.

ORANGE AND GRAPEFRUIT COCKTAIL

Cut out segments from a fresh grapefruit and orange and put in a bowl. Chop each segment and pile the pieces back into the empty grapefruit shells. Put into the fridge and take out 30 minutes before needed.

Fish

BAKED FISH

(serves 4)

2 tbsp olive oil	Lemon juice
750 g/1½ lb cod steaks	Parsley
Freshly ground black pepper	

Put half the olive oil in a casserole dish, add the fish and season with black pepper. Sprinkle the remainder of the oil and some lemon juice over the fish and bake at 200°C/ 400°F/Gas Mark 6 until tender. Garnish with chopped parsley.

Serve with spring greens and a tomato and onion salad.

SEA BASS WITH TARRAGON

(serves 4)

2 onions, sliced	Juice of 1 lemon
2 cloves garlic, crushed	1 kg/2 lb sea bass steaks
4 tbsp olive oil	Freshly ground black pepper
1 large glass dry white wine	Parsley
Bay leaf	
1 tbsp chopped fresh tarragon	

Fry the sliced onions together with the crushed garlic in a pan in the olive oil, adding the wine, bay leaf and tarragon.

Pour the lemon juice over the fish steaks and then the sauce.
Season with pepper and garnish with chopped parsley. Bake
in casserole dish (without covering) for 35 minutes at
180°C/350°F/Gas Mark 4.

BAKED MACKEREL WITH TOMATO SAUCE

(serves 4)

4 mackerel	2 tbsp olive oil
1 lemon	250 g/8 oz/1 cup
Freshly ground black	tomatoes, skinned and
pepper	chopped
A few sprigs fresh dill	1 garlic clove, chopped

Put the mackerel on baking foil with lemon rind, black
pepper and fresh dill.

Fold to make a parcel and bake for 40–45 minutes at
180°C/350°F/Gas Mark 4.

Meanwhile, warm the olive oil in a pan and add the
tomatoes and garlic clove. Cook gently for 20–30 minutes.
Pour the tomatoes over the mackerel when baked.

Serve with fresh spinach and cauliflower.

GREY MULLET

Lay each grey mullet on a piece of foil. Place a few sprigs
of dill and lemon rind inside the fish. Sprinkle lemon juice
over it. Bake slowly for 20 minutes on 180°C/350°F/Gas
Mark 4.

The same method can be used for a piece of salmon or
salmon trout. A whole fish will take longer to cook.

Serve with two green vegetables.

Mediterranean fish casserole

(serves 4)

1 large courgette	4 haddock fillets (about
500 g/1 lb leeks	750 g/1½ lb total
1 large green pepper, cut	weight)
in slices	Chopped parsley
250 g/8 oz/1 cup	1 tbsp lemon juice
tomatoes, chopped	
Freshly ground black	
pepper	

Chop the courgette and leeks into 2.5 cm/1 inch pieces and cook in a wok with the sliced pepper. Add the tomatoes and black pepper. Place in a casserole dish and lay the haddock fillets on top. Sprinkle with chopped parsley and lemon juice and bake for 20 minutes with the lid on. Remove the lid and cook for a further 10 minutes.

Serve on a bed of spinach.

Haddock florentine

(serves 4)

4 haddock fillets (750 g/	Pinch nutmeg
1½ lb total weight)	25 g/1 oz Edam cheese,
750 g/1½ lb fresh	grated
spinach	
Freshly ground black	
pepper	

Poach the haddock fillets in water, being careful not to overcook them. Steam the spinach and drain well. Make a bed of spinach in an ovenproof dish and lay the fish on top. Season with the pepper and nutmeg. Sprinkle grated Edam cheese on top. Place under the grill just till the cheese browns.

Chicken

BAKED GINGERED CHICKEN

(serves 4)

1 tbsp soy sauce	2 tsp grated fresh root
2 tbsp dry white wine	ginger
2 orange slices	4 chicken breast fillets
1 garlic clove, crushed	

Mix the soy sauce, white wine, orange slices, crushed garlic and grated ginger together and pour over the chicken fillets in a baking dish. Put a lid on the baking dish and leave to marinate for 3–4 hours.

Bake for 40 minutes at 200°C/400°F/Gas Mark 6.

Baste the chicken whilst cooking and turn once.

CHICKEN BREAST FILLETS IN MUSTARD

(serves 4)

2 tbsp olive oil	1 clove garlic, crushed
Few drops Worcestershire	Freshly ground black
sauce	pepper
1 tsp Dijon mustard	4 chicken breast fillets

Mix the olive oil, Worcestershire sauce, mustard, garlic and black pepper. Rub this mixture over the chicken breast fillets and bake for 40 minutes at 200°C/400°F/Gas Mark 6.

This sauce adds a little variety to chicken breast fillets.

CHICKEN WITH MUSTARD AND YOGURT

(serves 4)

Juice of 1 lemon	15 cl/¼ pint/½ cup
175 g/6 oz/¾ cup	natural low-fat yogurt
wholegrain mustard	Continental (flat-leafed)
4 chicken pieces	parsley for garnish
Freshly ground black	
pepper	

Sprinkle the lemon juice and wholegrain mustard over the chicken pieces in a baking dish. Season with black pepper and cook for 35 minutes at 200°C/400°F/Gas Mark 6. Turn the chicken once and baste well.

Turn out the chicken pieces onto a serving dish. Stir the yogurt into the cooking juices left in the dish and stir continuously, over low heat, for 2 minutes. Spoon this sauce over the chicken pieces.

Garnish with continental parsley and serve with courgettes and mange-touts.

CHICKEN CASSEROLE

(serves 4)

1.5 kg/3 lb chicken pieces, skin removed	1 bay leaf
	2 tbsp rosemary
250 g/8 oz celery, cut in chunks	2 cloves garlic, crushed
	Freshly ground black pepper
250 g/8 oz carrots, cut in chunks	Juice of 1 lemon
1 medium leek, cut in chunks	Chopped parsley for garnish

Place in a large pan the chicken, celery, carrots and leek. Add the herbs, garlic, black pepper and lemon juice. Add water to cover, bring to the boil, then lower heat and simmer gently, with the lid on, for 1–1½ hours, until the meat is tender.

Serve the chicken sprinkled with parsley.

Don't throw away the liquid that the chicken was cooked in. Cool it, then skim it and use for stock.

SPICED CHICKEN IN YOGURT

(serves 4)

4 chicken breast fillets	2 tsp turmeric
1 cm/$\frac{1}{2}$ inch piece of fresh root ginger, peeled and chopped	1 garlic clove, crushed
	Fresh coriander, chopped
	30 cl/$\frac{1}{2}$ pint/$1\frac{1}{4}$ cups
1 tsp chilli powder	low-fat natural yogurt

Prick the chicken breasts. Mix together the ginger, chilli powder, turmeric, garlic, coriander and yogurt. Pour this mixture over the chicken and leave in the fridge to marinate overnight. Bake the chicken in the oven at 190°C/375°F/Gas Mark 5 for 50 minutes, basting regularly and adding more yogurt as it cooks.

Pour over all the juices from the roasting tin when you serve the chicken.

SWEET CHICKEN

(serves 4)

3 tbsp olive oil	3 tbsp honey
1 onion, sliced thinly	Grated rind of 1 lemon
Freshly ground black pepper	A few leaves of fresh sage
	1 glass dry white wine
4 chicken breast fillets	

Heat the olive oil in a wok and fry the onions until they are transparent. Season with pepper. Lay the chicken breasts in an ovenproof dish, scatter the onions over them. Warm the honey, lemon rind and sage in a small saucepan and pour over the chicken. Bake in the oven at 180°C/350°F/Gas Mark 4 for 30 minutes. Pour the wine into the casserole dish and continue to bake until the chicken is soft (10–15 minutes more).

Serve with a dark green leafy vegetable and cauliflower.

CHICKEN KEBABS

(serves 4)

2 tbsp olive oil
1 garlic clove, crushed
4 tbsp lemon juice
1 tbsp chopped rosemary
Freshly ground black
  pepper

500 g/1 lb chicken fillets,
  cut into cubes
1 large onion, cut into
  large chunks

Mix together in a bowl the olive oil, garlic, 2 tbsp lemon juice, the rosemary and pepper, and pour this marinade over the chicken pieces. Leave for 3 hours.

Thread the chicken and onion pieces onto four skewers. Sprinkle with a pinch of salt and grill for 10 minutes on each side. Sprinkle with the remaining lemon juice after cooking.

Vegetables

JACKET POTATOES

These are a meal in themselves. They just need to be scrubbed well then pricked a few times with a fork so they don't burst in the oven.

Bake them at 200°C/400°F/Gas Mark 6, for 1 hour. The skins should be crispy and the insides soft, so they must be baked in the oven. Cooking them in the microwave won't leave them crisp. Add toppings (see below) but no butter – some fromage frais with chives tastes good and is not full of fat. Serve with vegetables or a salad.

JACKET POTATO TOPPINGS

Fromage frais – add chopped chives and parsley.

Sardines, mashed in their own tomato juice, sprinkled with parsley.

Drained tuna fish – add chunks of celery and dress with olive oil and lemon juice. Add chopped parsley.

Tinned sweetcorn, drained and mixed with frozen peas and chopped parsley.

Sliced tomatoes and sliced onion rings, dressed with olive oil and garnished with parsley.

Grated carrots and cold cooked lentils dressed with olive oil and a squeeze of lemon and garnished with parsley.

Low-fat curd cheese with herbs.

Chicken and sweetcorn, with green and red pepper rings, spring onion and chopped parsley.

Leeks and carrots, diced and dressed with olive oil, lemon juice, and chopped parsley.

Kidney beans dressed with vinaigrette, spring onions and parsley.

Ratatouille.

Green bean salad (see recipe, page 139).

Mushroom and peppers with chopped parsley.

Lentils and tuna.

Vegetable curry (see recipe, page 128).

Be sure to have a dark green leafy vegetable with your potato and some fresh fruit to follow.

BAKED POTATO AND RED CABBAGE

(serves 4)

½ red cabbage, sliced	1 tbsp vinegar
1 tsp demerara sugar	Freshly ground black
1 large cooking apple, peeled and chopped	pepper (optional)
Juice of 1 orange	4 large baking potatoes

Place the sliced red cabbage in a pan with the sugar, apple, orange juice and vinegar. You can also add some ground black pepper. Add a very little water. Cook on low light for 1 hour, watching to make sure it does not burn. Add a little more water if necessary.

Eat with crisp baked potatoes.

CHICORY PROVENÇALE

(serves 4)

4 heads chicory	Freshly ground black
1 tbsp olive oil	pepper
1 onion, chopped	Chopped parsley for
1 garlic clove, chopped	garnish
4 tomatoes, skinned and chopped	6 black olives, halved and stoned
1 tbsp tomato purée	

Boil the chicory until *al dente* (still firm when bitten). Drain and place in a casserole dish. Stir fry in olive oil the chopped onion and garlic. When they become transparent add the tomatoes, tomato purée and black pepper. Cook for 1 minute, then pour over the chicory and bake for 15 minutes at 190°C/375°F/Gas Mark 5. Garnish with chopped parsley and olive halves.

This dish is nice with grilled fish or as a lunchtime snack by itself with a green salad.

BEAN BAKE

(serves 4)

2 garlic cloves, chopped	1 × 200 g/7 oz tin baked
500 g/1 lb onions, thinly	beans
sliced	1 × 200 g/7 oz tin butter
2 tbsp olive oil	beans, drained
1 red pepper, sliced	1 × 200 g/7 oz tin
1 green pepper, sliced	tomatoes
whole cauliflower, broken	2 tbsp tomato purée
into florets	1 tbsp paprika

Cook the garlic and onion in the olive oil until transparent. Add the red and green peppers and the cauliflower florets and cook for 1 minute. Add the baked beans, butter beans, tomatoes, tomato purée and paprika. Simmer for 10–12 minutes. Serve hot or cold.

HOT OR COLD MÉLANGE OF VEGETABLES VINAIGRETTE

(serves 4)

This is a very easy dish to make, it is also tasty and nutritious. The vegetables can be varied according to choice.

250 g/8 oz frozen broad	*Dressing:*
beans, frozen peas,	Olive oil
frozen french beans,	Lemon juice
frozen cauliflower or	Freshly ground black
sweetcorn	pepper

Cook all the frozen vegetables in boiling water, till *al dente* (still firm when bitten). Drain well. Mix together the dressing ingredients (use approximately $\frac{1}{3}$ lemon juice to $\frac{2}{3}$ olive oil). Toss the vegetables in the dressing.

You can sprinkle some grated Edam cheese over the vegetables and brown under the grill if this is your main meal of the day.

Vegetable curry

(serves 4)

2 tbsp olive oil
2 garlic cloves, chopped
1 medium onion, chopped
3 tsp medium/hot curry powder
2 potatoes, peeled and chopped
2 carrots, peeled and sliced
1 cauliflower broken into florets
1 green pepper, seeded and chopped
250 g/8 oz/1 cup tomatoes, skinned and chopped
15 cl/$\frac{1}{4}$ pint/$\frac{1}{2}$ cup water
30 cl/$\frac{1}{2}$ pint/$1\frac{1}{4}$ cups low-fat natural yogurt

Heat the olive oil in a saucepan and add the garlic, onion and curry powder. Stir this mixture for 3 minutes continuously over low heat. Add the potatoes, carrots, cauliflower and the green pepper and stir them to coat them with the mixture. Then add the tomatoes and about 15 cl/$\frac{1}{4}$ pint/$\frac{1}{2}$ cup water. Bring to the boil and then simmer for 30 minutes. Pour into dish and mix in the yogurt before serving.

Serve on a bed of wholegrain rice.

Cabbage with caraway seeds

White cabbage
Caraway seeds to taste
Paprika
2 tbsp olive oil
2 tsp white wine vinegar
Freshly ground black pepper

Wash and drain the cabbage, then shred finely. Sprinkle the caraway seeds over the cabbage. Mix together the paprika, olive oil and wine vinegar, season with black pepper and pour this dressing over the cabbage.

FENNEL AND EDAM BAKE

4 heads of fennel, cut in quarters
Black pepper
4 tbsp grated Edam cheese
Chopped parsley for garnish

Boil fennel until *al dente* (still firm when bitten). Place in a casserole dish rubbed with olive oil (to make sure the fennel won't stick). Grind black pepper over the fennel and sprinkle on the Edam cheese. Bake in the oven at 180°C/350°F/Gas Mark 4 until the cheese has turned brown. Garnish with chopped parsley.

Eat with a tomato salad in olive oil and lemon juice sprinkled with chopped parsley.

AUBERGINES WITH TOMATOES

Aubergines can be grilled without fat. Slice them in 1 cm/ ½ inch slices and grill till brown. Eat them as they are or place them in a casserole dish with a layer of sliced tomatoes on top. Add 1 tablespoon of olive oil and brown in the oven.

CAROTTES RÂPÉES

Grate your carrots just before eating otherwise you lose most of the goodness.

Grate some carrots. Sprinkle with lemon juice. Add olive oil. You can add raisins or sultanas if you wish.

Grains and pasta

GREENBRAE RICE

(serves 4)

1 small onion, chopped
coarsely
50 g/2 oz slivered
almonds
50 g/2 oz/¼ cup olive oil
spread, melted
250 g/8 oz/1 cup
wholegrain rice

60 cl/1 pint/2½ cups
hot chicken stock
(1 chicken cube)
50 g/2 oz/¼ cup sultanas
(golden raisins)

Heat the oven to 190°C/375°F/Gas Mark 5. Sauté the onion and almonds in the olive oil spread until golden, add the rice, mix and sauté for a few minutes longer. Pour on the hot stock, stir, then add the sultanas. Place in a casserole dish and bake for 30 minutes.

TABBOULEH

(serves 4)

125 g/4 oz/½ cup
cracked wheat
1 beef tomato, seeded and
chopped
¼ cucumber, chopped
8 large spring onions,
sliced

Chopped basil
Fresh coriander leaves
2 tbsp olive oil
2 tbsp lemon juice
Freshly ground black
pepper
1 Webbs lettuce

Place the cracked wheat in a bowl covered with cold water. After about 30 minutes drain thoroughly. Mix in the chopped tomato, chopped cucumber, spring onions, herbs, olive oil, lemon juice and black pepper. Line a salad bowl with lettuce leaves and spoon in the tabbouleh.

Wholewheat pasta spirals with tuna

(serves 4)

250 g/8 oz/1 cup
  wholewheat pasta
  spirals or shapes
1 × 200 g/7 oz tin of
  tuna, canned in oil
1 medium onion,
  chopped
1 clove garlic, chopped

1 × 250 g/8 oz tin
  tomatoes (without
  sugar)
Chopped parsley, for
  garnish
Freshly ground black
  pepper

Cook the pasta in boiling water until it is *al dente* (still slightly firm when bitten).

Drain the oil from the tin of tuna into a frying pan. Fry the onion and garlic gently in the oil until golden, not brown. Discard the garlic. Add the tuna and mash with a fork to break it up. Add the tomatoes and let the mixture simmer until slightly reduced.

Pour the sauce over the pasta and sprinkle with chopped parsley. Season with black pepper.

Pasta salad

(serves 4)

250 g/8 oz/1 cup pasta
  shapes
2 peppers, sliced
2 carrots, grated
2 large tomatoes, sliced
2 large spring onions,
  sliced
125 g/4 oz/1 cup
  mushrooms, chopped

2 tbsp olive oil
2 tbsp lemon juice
Freshly ground black
  pepper
Chopped chives and
  parsley, for garnish

Cook the pasta until it is *al dente* and allow to get cold. Mix above vegetables together and pour over the pasta. Dress with olive oil and lemon juice, season with black pepper and garnish with the chives and parsley.

PEPPER SAUCE FOR PASTA

(serves 4)

1 medium size onion,
finely chopped
1 or 2 garlic cloves (to
taste), crushed
Olive oil
1 green pepper, seeded
and cut in rings
1 red pepper, seeded and
cut in rings

4 tinned tomatoes (no
added sugar)
Freshly ground black
pepper
Chopped continental
(flat-leafed) parsley

Fry the finely chopped onion and the garlic in olive oil. Add
the pepper rings and the tomatoes. Cook for 4–5 minutes
until the peppers are softish. Mix the sauce into the pasta
and add ground black pepper. Garnish with continental
parsley.

ONION SAUCE

(serves 4)

3 or 4 onions, cut into
rings
1 or 2 garlic cloves
2 tbsp olive oil
6–8 tbsp water
15 cl/¼ pint/½ cup
vegetable stock

2 tbsp tomato purée
Freshly ground black
pepper
Fresh basil, chopped

Put the onion rings and garlic in a pan with the olive oil and
4 tbsp water. Cook gently for 20 minutes, stirring continuously. When the onion is soft mix together the vegetable
stock, tomato purée and 3 tbsp water in a small bowl. Add
this to the onions, stir well, cook for 5 minutes, then add to
your pasta shapes, seasoning with ground black pepper and
chopped basil.

Mushroom sauce

(serves 4)

1 medium onion, sliced	8 tbsp water
2 tbsp olive oil	Freshly ground black
2 cloves garlic, chopped	pepper
500 g/1 lb/4 cups	Chopped parsley for
mushrooms, chopped	garnish

Fry the onion in the olive oil and stir in the garlic. Add the chopped mushrooms and the water. Put lid on the pan or wok and leave to cook for 10 minutes, stirring occasionally.

Mix all the ingredients together. Spoon over the pasta, add ground black pepper and chopped parsley.

Fennel sauce for pasta

(serves 4)

1 small fennel bulb, trimmed
1 small eating apple, peeled and cored
Juice of 1 lemon
1 tsp chopped fresh dill

Put all the ingredients in a blender and purée until smooth. Serve on pasta.

Easy tomato sauce for pasta

A really easy recipe for a tomato sauce to throw over your pasta dishes is made with fresh tomatoes, chopped, skinned (in boiling water) and melted in olive oil. When they are still firm (don't let them get mushy), add black pepper and fresh basil.

TOMATO SAUCE

1 medium onion,
  chopped
1 clove garlic, chopped
Fresh basil leaves,
  chopped
2 tbsp olive oil
500 g/1 lb/2 cups
  tomatoes, skinned and
  chopped

1 tsp tomato purée
Freshly ground black
  pepper
Chopped parsley for
  garnish

Cook the onion, garlic and chopped basil leaves in the olive
oil for a minute or two, then add the chopped tomatoes,
tomato purée and black pepper and cook on a very low heat
for 40 minutes. There is no need to sieve before serving.

This sauce is good on pasta dishes – just garnish with
parsley.

Salads

Salads are best made when you need them and not left
hanging around, so try to make no more than 30 minutes
before needed and cover them loosely with clingfilm. Dress
them at the table.

Colourful salads on white plates or bowls look very
attractive but don't try too many flavours at the same time
and don't end up with mushy ingredients because you have
shred or grated too finely.

Pat dry your salad ingredients. If you use a colander for
draining, remember not to use a metal one which may make
your salad taste metallic. Use nylon mesh instead.

Garnish, as often as you can, with fresh parsley or
continental parsley, which you can either buy or grow – it
has very prettily shaped leaves. Use fresh, rather than dried,
herbs whenever possible. Also chop spring onion or garlic
into every salad.

Eat the vegetable salads with a dressing made from equal quantities of olive oil and lemon juice, seasoned with black pepper and garnished with chopped parsley as a snack lunch with stoneground wholemeal bread and olive oil spread.

BROCCOLI AND CAULIFLOWER SALAD

Cauliflower florets
Broccoli florets
Olive oil and lemon juice
Freshly ground black
   pepper

Chopped parsley for
   garnish

Cook the cauliflower and broccoli florets until *al dente* (still slightly firm when bitten). Drain arid dress with olive oil, lemon juice and black pepper. Scatter with chopped parsley. Eat hot or cold.

ORANGE AND WATERCRESS SALAD

(serves 4)

4 bunches watercress,
   well washed
Lettuce leaves (a mixture
   of varieties)
3 small oranges, peeled
   and divided into
   segments

Olive oil, lemon juice,
   black pepper
Chopped parsley for
   garnish

Place the orange segments round a salad of watercress and lettuce leaves. Dress with olive oil, lemon juice and black pepper, garnish with chopped parsley.

Try variation with endive, watercress and orange segments, add sliced onion rings and chopped parsley.

HOT SCALLOP SALAD

(serves 2)

Baby lettuce leaves	4 mushrooms, sliced
4 king scallops	1 tomato, skinned and
2 tbsp olive oil	chopped
Freshly ground black	1 tbsp chopped parsley
pepper	1 tbsp balsamic vinegar

Lay the lettuce leaves in a bowl. Put the scallops into an ovenproof dish, dribble over 1 tbsp of olive oil and some black pepper. Grill for 3 minutes on each side until opaque.

Meanwhile slice the mushrooms and fry in the remaining olive oil for 4 minutes.

Whilst the scallops are still hot, stir in the tomato, parsley and balsamic vinegar. Spoon the scallops onto the lettuce, then spoon on the mushrooms, pour over all the cooking juices and serve.

TOMATO SALAD

Slice (but not too finely) some firm ripe tomatoes. Pour over olive oil and lemon juice. Season with black pepper and garnish with parsley. Place thinly sliced onions or chopped spring onions on top of the tomato slices and add some chopped basil, as a variation.

ORANGE AND FENNEL SALAD

    1 large fennel bulb
    2 large oranges
    Olive oil, lemon juice, black pepper
    Chopped parsley for garnish

Remove the core from the fennel bulb and slice it (but not too finely). Peel and slice the oranges and surround the fennel with the segments. Add the dressing of olive oil, lemon juice and black pepper and sprinkle with parsley.

This salad can be arranged on a bed of lettuce or fennel leaves.

TUNA RICE SALAD

Cook wholegrain rice and add flaked tuna fish, sweetcorn, peas, spring onions, red pepper rings, black olives. Dress with olive oil, lemon juice and black pepper, garnish with lots of chopped parsley.

COURGETTE SALAD

>   Courgettes
>   Olive oil, lemon juice
>   Freshly ground black pepper
>   Chopped parsley for garnish

Boil the courgettes until *al dente* (still slightly firm when bitten), drain, chop and pour over your usual olive oil and lemon juice dressing. Season with black pepper. Garnish with chopped parsley. Eat hot or cold.

Why not experiment with salads? Here are a few ideas of some ingredients to throw together:

- green beans, tomatoes, lettuce, fennel, black olives, tiny slices of feta cheese

- spinach and avocado pear

- celery with fromage frais, garnished with mint

- endive and fresh pear, decorated with grapes

- grated carrots and a sprinkling of sultanas, dressed with olive oil, lemon juice, black pepper

- curd cheese with fresh figs

- cottage cheese and stoned green olives

- green, red and yellow pepper rings with sweetcorn and chopped parsley

KIDNEY BEANS WITH CHOPPED ONION AND
BROCCOLI FLORETS

(serves 2)

1 small tin kidney beans,
  drained
Broccoli florets, cooked
  and drained
2 large spring onions,
  sliced

Olive oil, lemon juice,
  black pepper
Chopped parsley for
  garnish

Mix together the kidney beans, broccoli florets and spring
onions. Dress and add the chopped parsley.

WATERCRESS AND MUSHROOM SALAD

125 g/4 oz/1 cup
  mushrooms
Juice of 1 lemon
2 spring onions, sliced
Chives, chopped

Bunch of watercress,
  chopped
4 tbsp low-fat fromage
  frais

Slice the mushrooms and sprinkle with lemon juice. Add
spring onions, chives and chopped watercress to the low-fat
fromage frais, stir well and pour over the mushrooms.

CHICORY SALAD WITH LOW-FAT YOGURT

Chicory
1 × 15 cl/¼ pint carton of low-fat natural yogurt
Lemon juice
Mint

Chop the chicory. Mix the yogurt with lemon juice, add
chopped mint and pour over the chicory.

Pepper salad

(serves 4)

Grill 2 large green and 2 large red peppers until the skin blisters and turns black. Peel, then cut the peppers into strips. Garnish with stoned black olives. Dress with olive oil, lemon juice and black pepper and garnish with chopped parsley. Serve with sliced tomato and onion rings.

Green salad

Lettuce leaves (several varieties)
Celery, thinly sliced
Spring onions, sliced
Watercress, chopped
Cucumber, sliced
Chicory
Endive
Green pepper, cut into rings
Olive oil, lemon juice
Chopped parsley for garnish
Freshly ground black pepper

Arrange different types of green lettuce on a plate and add thin slices of celery, sliced spring onions and chopped watercress. Add sliced cucumber, chicory leaves, endive and pepper rings. Dress with olive oil and lemon juice and add chopped parsley and black pepper.

Green bean salad

French beans, topped and tailed
Sesame oil
Sesame seeds

Put the french beans into boiling water for 2 minutes, drain and plunge into cold water to stop them cooking. When drained, put into bowl and dribble with sesame oil. Toast some sesame seeds in a medium oven for 5–10 minutes and then scatter over the beans.

STUFFED PEPPER SALAD

(serves 2)

2 green peppers
250 g/8 oz/2 cups
  cooked wholegrain rice
250 g/8 oz/1 cup
  mushrooms, sliced
1 small tin sweetcorn
  (without added sugar)

Olive oil, lemon juice,
  black pepper
Chopped parsley for
  garnish

Remove the seeds from each pepper and cut in half lengthways. Fill each half pepper with cooked rice, sliced mushrooms, and sweetcorn. Dress with olive oil, lemon juice and black pepper and garnish with chopped parsley.
  Serve with salad.

TOMATO AND FENNEL SALAD

2 fennel bulbs
4 tomatoes

Dressing:
15 cl/¼ pint/½ cup low-
  fat fromage frais

Olive oil, lemon juice
Basil leaves and chopped
  chives

Slice the fennel and tomatoes and place on a plate. Mix together lemon juice and olive oil with the low-fat fromage frais. Pour this over the fennel and tomatoes and sprinkle on the basil leaves and chopped chives.

KOHLRABI SALAD

(serves 4)

2 kohlrabi bulbs
Olive oil
Lemon juice
Freshly ground black
  pepper

Chopped parsley for
  garnish

Top and tail the kohlrabi bulbs and grate them coarsely. Sprinkle lemon juice over the grated kohlrabi. Pour over the olive oil and chopped parsley.

MEDITERRANEAN FISH SALAD

(serves 4)

500 g/1 lb haddock
1 red pepper, chopped
1 yellow pepper, chopped
1 green pepper, chopped
50 g/2 oz/¼ cup peas
2 large tomatoes, skinned and chopped
4 large spring onions, chopped
¼ cucumber, peeled and chopped

250 g/8 oz/1 cup wholegrain rice, cooked and cooled
Olive oil
1 tbsp white wine vinegar
1 clove garlic, crushed
Pinch of French mustard
Freshly ground black pepper
Chopped parsley for garnish

Steam the haddock then flake and mix with the peppers, peas, tomatoes, spring onions and cucumber. Mix into the rice.

Stir all the ingredients together carefully without breaking the haddock into too small pieces. Make a dressing with the oil, wine vinegar, garlic, mustard and black pepper in a bowl. Pour the dressing over the salad and add chopped parsley.

SALADE NIÇOISE

(serves 4)

Lettuce leaves
Cold new potatoes in their skins, halved
4 tomatoes, cut in quarters
125 g/4 oz/1 cup cooked french beans, cut in chunks
1 green pepper, sliced in rings
1 red pepper, sliced in rings
¼ cucumber, cut in cubes

2 hard-boiled eggs, cut in quarters
1 × 200 g/7 oz tin of tuna in oil
8 stoned black olives

Dressing:
Olive oil
Lemon juice
Freshly ground black pepper
Chopped parsley for garnish

Line a salad bowl with lettuce leaves. Place the vegetables and quarters of egg in the bowl. Drain the tuna, flake into small chunks and add to the bowl. Place the stoned black olives on top. Make a dressing with olive oil, lemon juice and black pepper and pour over. Garnish with chopped parsley.

SALAD FROM THE MIDDLE EAST

(serves 4)

1 large red pepper	500 g/1 lb/1½ cups
1 large green pepper	tomatoes, skinned,
	seeded and chopped
Dressing:	
Olive oil	Freshly ground black
Lemon juice	pepper
Crushed garlic clove	Chopped parsley for
½ tsp ground cinnamon	garnish
2 tbsp chopped coriander	
leaves	

De-seed the peppers and cut into quarters. Place under a hot grill, skin side up, until the skin blisters. Peel off the skin. Chop the peppers.

Mix together the tomatoes and peppers. Mix together the dressing ingredients, pour over the salad and garnish with chopped parsley.

MOZZARELLA SALAD

(serves 4)

2 ripe avocados	Olive oil
4 tomatoes, sliced	Freshly ground black
250 g/8 oz mozzarella	pepper
cheese, sliced	Chopped parsley for
Lemon juice	garnish

Remove the stones from the avocados and halve. Skin then cut into slices. Arrange alternating slices of tomato, mozzarella and avocado on four plates. Dress with lemon juice and olive oil, season with black pepper and garnish with chopped parsley.

MUSHROOMS À LA GRECQUE

(serves 6)

1 tbsp lemon juice	750 g/1½ lb fresh
1 garlic clove	mushrooms
1 onion, chopped	500 g/1 lb fresh
Freshly ground black	tomatoes, skinned
pepper	Chopped parsley

In a saucepan heat the lemon juice, garlic clove, onion and a little black pepper. Bring to the boil, add the mushrooms and tomatoes and simmer.

After 5 minutes, turn out and leave until cold. Sprinkle on chopped parsley and serve on a bed of mixed lettuce leaves.

Sauces and dressings

If you want a sauce that you can add easily to plain grilled fish, try olive oil with lemon juice, parsley and chervil.

RED PEPPER DIP

2 red peppers	2 tbsp olive oil
125 g/4 oz/⅓ cup feta	Freshly ground black
cheese	pepper
125 g/4 oz/⅓ cup	
low-fat cream cheese	

Grill the peppers until the skin blisters, then peel off the skin. Chop then put them into the blender. Process the peppers with the cheeses and dribble in the olive oil. Season with pepper.

This dip is a nice change to fromage frais or curd cheese and goes well with all raw vegetables. You can also use it as a pâté on wholemeal toast.

Cucumber and yogurt sauce

½ cucumber, grated	Parsley
1 × 150 g/5 oz carton low-fat natural yogurt	Freshly ground black pepper
2 tbsp lemon juice	Watercress for garnish

Blend all the ingredients together in a blender, except for the watercress. This dressing is good with fish. Garnish with watercress.

French dressing with basil

3 tbsp olive oil	1 garlic clove, crushed
1 tbsp lemon juice	Crushed basil leaves
¼ tsp French mustard	
Freshly ground black pepper	

Mix all the ingredients together in a screw-top jar and keep this in the fridge to be available each time you want a ready-made French dressing. Shake the jar to mix the dressing when needed, and top up as necessary.

Yogurt and dill dressing

1 tsp Dijon mustard	1 × 150 g/5 oz low-fat natural yogurt
2 tbsp chopped dill	Freshly ground black pepper
2 tbsp chopped continental (flat-leafed) parsley	

Stir the Dijon mustard, dill and continental parsley into the yogurt. Add black pepper.
    This dressing is nice over fish.

MARINADE FOR CHICKEN

(for 4 chicken fillets)

15 cl/¼ pint/½ cup olive oil
1 garlic clove, crushed
Black pepper
2 tbsp lemon juice

1 tbsp chopped rosemary
1 tbsp chopped tarragon
1 tbsp chopped basil
1 tbsp chopped chives

Mix all the ingredients together.

MARINADE FOR FISH

(for 4 pieces of fish)

15 cl/¼ pint/½ cup olive oil
2 tbsp chopped tarragon
2 tbsp lemon juice
2 tbsp white wine

Mix all the ingredients together.

With both these marinades you can sprinkle on the chopped herbs after cooking your chicken fillets or fish.

Desserts

MAKE YOUR OWN YOGURT

Nutritious and easy to make.

1.2 l/2 pints/5 cups low-fat calcium-enriched milk
3 tbsp low-fat natural yogurt

Bring the milk to the boil in a saucepan, then cool. Add the yogurt, stirring well. Leave to stand for at least 10–14 hours somewhere warm, e.g. in an airing cupboard or near your central heating boiler. The mixture will thicken and should then be transferred to the fridge.

BAKED APPLES

(serves 4)

> 4 cooking apples
> 125 g/4 oz/1 cup sultanas
> 4 tbsp water

Core and prick the apples. Put in a microwave dish and pour the water round. Fill the cavities with sultanas.

Cook the apples for 2 minutes on high. Remove from the oven and leave to stand for 3 minutes, covered.

Eat with low-fat natural yogurt or fromage frais.

FROMAGE FRAIS WITH WHEATGERM

Add some chopped nuts and raisins to a bowl of low-fat fromage frais topped with wheatgerm. Serve chilled.

BLACKBERRIES WITH REDCURRANTS

(serves 4)

> 250 g/8 oz/2 cups redcurrants
> 250 g/8 oz/2 cups blackberries

Strip the redcurrants from their stems by running a fork along the string of currants. Add the blackberries. If you need to, add liquid low-calorie sweetener. Serve with low-fat natural yogurt.

Try different varieties of berries and currants when they are in season.

BANANA CRUNCH

(serves 2)

> 1 large banana, sliced
> Low-fat natural fromage frais
> 6 tbsp fruit and nut muesli
> Cinnamon

Mix the fromage frais with a pinch of cinnamon. Pour over the sliced banana and top with the fruit and nut muesli.

RHUBARB AND BANANA BAKE

(serves 1)

Cook some rhubarb, cut into 2.5 cm/1 inch chunks, with the juice and grated rind of an orange or lemon. Add one banana per person, sliced, and cover with microwave film. Cook on high for 1 minute.

If you are making 500 g/1 lb rhubarb, cook this first for 4 minutes and when you are ready to divide it up for a dessert, put some into a dish with the sliced banana and heat for 1 minute on high.

Sprinkle with cinnamon (optional).

BANANAS OR PEACHES IN ORANGE JUICE

(serves 4)

    4 bananas or peaches, peeled and cut into thick slices
    Grated rind and juice of 2 oranges
    50 g/1 oz flaked almonds, toasted, or muesli
    Natural low-fat yogurt (optional) to serve

Place the fruit in an ovenproof dish. Pour over the orange juice and the rind. Cover and bake in a pre-heated oven at 180°C/350°F/Gas Mark 4 for 15–20 minutes until fruit is just tender. Serve hot, sprinkled with toasted almonds or muesli and eat with yogurt, if liked.

REDCURRANTS AND MANGO WITH FROMAGE FRAIS

(serves 4)

    125–175 g/4–6 oz/1–1½ cups redcurrants
    1 large mango, sliced
    Low-fat fromage frais

Strip the redcurrants from their stems with a fork. Mix the redcurrants and slices of mango and serve with fromage frais.

The next three recipes are for delicious and refreshing desserts to serve when entertaining at home.

PEACHES WITH RASPBERRY SAUCE

(serves 6)

> 6 fresh peaches, peeled and sliced
> 750 g/1½ lbs fresh raspberries

Lay the peaches carefully on a platter. Purée the raspberries in a blender then pour the sauce over the peaches. Place in fridge, taking out half an hour before needed.

MELON WITH GRAPES

(serves 6)

> 2 ogen melons
> 500 g/1 lb seedless grapes, green and black varieties, skinned
> 1 tbsp lemon juice

Cut the melons horizontally and remove the seeds. Place a mixture of grapes in the melon halves. Sprinkle on the lemon juice. Put in fridge, covered. Take out half an hour before needed.

GRAPEFRUIT WITH RASPBERRIES

(serves 2)

> 1 grapefruit
> 125 g/4 oz/1 cup raspberries

Cut the grapefruit in half, remove the flesh and put in a bowl. Chop into pieces, put back into the shell and add the raspberries. Add any juice left in the bowl. Put in the fridge and take out half an hour before use.

Drinks

TOMATO JUICE

(This will make enough for three evenings)

This is the easy-to-make tomato juice which I suggest as a pick-you-up every night when you get in from the office. It is very refreshing and won't use up any of your alcohol allowance.

>   500 g/1 lb tomatoes, peeled and chopped
>   Freshly ground black pepper
>   Worcestershire sauce

Process the chopped tomatoes in a blender until you reach the consistency you like. Sieve and add black pepper and Worcestershire sauce, according to taste.

ORANGE AND LEMON DRINK

Try this as an alternative to your tomato juice in the evening. It is full of vitamin C.

>   2 oranges, quartered, pips removed
>   2 lemons, quartered, pips removed
>   1.2 l/2 pints/5 cups water

Process oranges, lemons and water in a blender for 10 seconds on fast.

FINAL QUIZ

===

Let's see how you're doing:

1. Which colour bread, rice and pasta will you choose?

2. Why?

3. Am I better off going without breakfast?

4. What will you do when the snack-laden office trolley arrives?

5. What exercise, if any, have you taken before arriving at the office?

6. How many times a week, and for how long, is it necessary to exercise in order to become fit and maintain fitness?

7. What should I do when I've picked up the children from school, given them their tea and feel ready to raid the fridge?

8. What sort of form should my shopping at the super-market take?

9. Why is eating fibre so good?

10. How can I avoid eating a bowl of peanuts with my drink at the wine bar?

11. Why is this plan *not* a diet?

12. Can I expect to see results soon?

13. Why is it a good idea for all the family to follow the ideas in this book?

14. Which is the best way of cooking vegetables?

15. Why is eating raw vegetables and fruit so good for you?

16. Why the inclusion of foods rich in vitamin C?

17. What happens if I fail?

18. What sort of fats should I avoid?

19. How do I reduce the risk of having high cholesterol?

20. What dressings should you use in place of mayonnaise?

Scoring:

Possible score 65

55-65
You've really grasped the concept of enjoying your life, making the most of eating and exercising and enjoying them to the full. Congratulations!

45-55
Very good start – you're really on the way to leading a life you'll be happy with and you really want to succeed. Keep up the great work!

35-45
Maybe you just need to read the book again or concentrate on some of the points which you haven't quite grasped. Do try again!

25-35
You haven't quite grasped the concept – why not enrol a friend and go through the book together? It could be fun.

Less than 25
Are you sure you want to change? If yes, congratulations on admitting it. Just start again from Chapter 1, read a chapter a day and then practise what you read.

Good luck!

Answers

Score 3 points for every correct answer.

1. Brown every time!

2. Brown means the fibre has not been removed. Refining removes the valuable husk.

3. No, you need to eat breakfast to stave off the hunger pangs which would lead you to grabbing a snack mid-morning. Aim for a bowl of high-fibre cereal, porridge or muesli – slow-release foods which keep energy levels high.

4. Get out your carrots and/or a banana.

5. If you haven't been for an early morning swim or done a few minutes on the exercise bike, you should at least have got off the bus two stops before your destination and walked, or walked up the escalator and not taken the lift once at the office.

6. Twenty minutes three times a week is sufficient but you may wish to exercise for longer and more often.

7. You can have your half sandwich and fruit – specially designated for this danger time.

8. An organized form – with a list made up of all the foods and groups of foods suggested in the eating plan. If you have copied the suggested supermarket list, add an extra two bonus points.

9. Because foods high in fibre fill you up and leave you feeling full up for longer and make laxatives unnecessary.

10. By following the strategy suggested on page 39. Before leaving the office have your danger time allowance – in this way, you won't feel the need to indulge in a bowl of salty nuts and will be able to enjoy a proper evening meal when you leave the wine bar or pub.

11. This plan is not a diet because a 'diet' is something temporary – and what we're aiming at is a healthy lifestyle, with healthy eating and exercising, for life.

12. Yes. You'll not only look better but you'll feel better too, and have more zest for living.

13. As the eating plan is not a diet and is just a sensible way to eat and exercise, why shouldn't the whole family benefit?

14. Steaming, microwaving or boiling (3 extra points if you named all three ways).

15. Raw foods are more filling and satisfying than cooked; vegetables are more filling when they are raw; they increase your fibre level and reduce your cholesterol level, too. Raw food is delicious.

16. Vitamin C is extremely beneficial when you are withdrawing from tobacco. Foods rich in vitamin C also protect against heart disease. Foods rich in vitamin C give you extra energy – which you most certainly need to combat withdrawal symptoms. Make sure you eat lots of fruit, especially berries, tomatoes, vegetables and potatoes.

17. If you do have a temporary lapse, just start again.

18. You should avoid saturated fats because these are the fats which produce cholesterol and lead to heart disease.

19. By eating only unsaturated or monounsaturated fats, i.e. drink semi-skimmed or skimmed milk, use low-fat spread or one high in polyunsaturates, eat low-fat cheeses like cottage cheese, Edam or Gouda, low-fat curd cheese and fromage frais. By cutting off all fat from meat and eating chicken without the skin. By trying to eat only fish or poultry.

20. a) olive oil and lemon juice
    b) fromage frais, chives and lemon juice
    c) low-fat yogurt, chives and lemon juice

INDEX: GENERAL

INDEX: RECIPES

USEFUL ADDRESSES

ASH – Action on Smoking and Health
5/11 Mortimer Street
LONDON W1
071-935 3519

British Heart Foundation
14 Fitzhardinge Street
LONDON W1H 9PL
071-935 0185

British Medical Association
Tavistock Square
LONDON WC1H 9JP
071-387 4499

Cancer Research Campaign
Charles House
Lower Regent Street
LONDON SW1Y 4LR
071-839 2040

Cancer Research Campaign
350 North End Road
LONDON SW6 1NB
071-381 8485

Coronary Prevention Group
102 Gloucester Place
LONDON W1H 3DA
071-935 2887

Health Education Authority
Hamilton House
Mabledon Place
LONDON WC1
071-387 9528

Health Education Board for Scotland
Woodburn House
Canaan Lane
EDINBURGH EH10 4SG
031-447 8044

Health Promotion Agency for Northern Ireland
18 Ormeau Avenue
BELFAST BT2 8HS
0232 311611

Health Promotion Agency for Wales
Brunel House
8th Floor
2 Fitzalan Road
CARDIFF CF2 1EB
0222 472472

Imperial Cancer Research Fund
Lincolns Inn Fields
LONDON WC2
071-242 0200
Regional Offices
26 Victoria Road
SURBITON Surrey
081-390 6659

Marie Curie Cancer Care
28 Belgrave Square
LONDON W1X 8QG
071-235 3325

National Asthma Campaign
300 Upper Street
LONDON N1 2XX
071-226 2260

QUIT
102 Gloucester Place
LONDON W1H 3DA
071-487 2858

Royal College of General Practitioners
14 Princes Gate
LONDON SW7 1PU
071-581 3232

Royal Pharmaceutical Society
1 Lambeth High Street
LONDON SE1 7JR
071-735 9141

Stroke Association
123 Whitecross Street
LONDON EC1
071-490 7999